Be Your Own Lobbyist

How to Give Your Small Business Big Clout with State and Local Government

Amy H. Handlin

 PRAEGER

AN IMPRINT OF ABC-CLIO, LLC
Santa Barbara, California • Denver, Colorado • Oxford, England

Library of Congress Cataloging-in-Publication Data

Handlin, Amy H., 1956–
  Be your own lobbyist : how to give your small business big clout with state and local
government / Amy H. Handlin.
    p. cm.
  Includes bibliographical references and index.
  ISBN 978–0–313–38155–3 (hard copy : alk. paper) — ISBN 978–0–313–38156–0 (ebook)
1. Small business. 2. Lobbying. I. Title.
HD2341.H296 2010
659.2′93244—dc22   2010004270

ISBN: 978–0–313–38155–3
EISBN: 978–0–313–38156–0

14 13 12 11 10   1 2 3 4 5

This book is also available on the World Wide Web as an eBook.
Visit www.abc-clio.com for details.

Praeger
An Imprint of ABC-CLIO, LLC

ABC-CLIO, LLC
130 Cremona Drive, P.O. Box 1911
Santa Barbara, California 93116-1911

This book is printed on acid-free paper ∞

Manufactured in the United States of America

To David, Daniel, and Rebecca

Contents

Preface

Over the course of 20 years in state and local government, I have known countless strong, successful people who built formidable businesses but still felt powerless at City Hall. It never crossed their minds to challenge the conventional wisdom that government can only be influenced by big corporations, professional lobbyists, and multimillionaires.

That simply isn't true. Worse, it is a self-fulfilling prophecy. If you were convinced that no one would buy a certain product, how hard would you try to sell it?

This book is focused on lobbying officials in your town, county or state. Compared to those in Washington, local decision-makers are physically closer to their constituents as well as more directly involved with community life. It's no accident that businesspeople routinely view them with trepidation: for better or worse, their administrative and regulatory decisions reach into every corner of the marketplace.

But these officials are also more accessible than their federal counterparts, more sensitive to hometown criticism, and, frankly, more vulnerable in local elections. Ironically, many state and local officials are more fearful of you than you are of them. My goal is to help you strengthen the muscle you have always had—whether or not you have ever flexed it.

When you lobby, it is (normally) unreasonable to demand a particular decision, action, or vote. But every public official owes you clarity, honesty, and respect:

Clarity—in explaining what is feasible;

Honesty—in acknowledging what is not; and

Respect—for your ability to understand the difference.

Don't hesitate to demand your due.

At the same time, it is your responsibility to be an educated, realistic advocate. Even the most diligent, well-intentioned official can't give the right answer to the wrong question. He won't be able to act outside his jurisdiction or resolve a matter in which he has no say. Conversely, a lazy or inept official might blame his own failures on the nature or imprecision of your request. This book will also help you avoid such common pitfalls.

Of course, there are no guarantees in lobbying. Getting an official to go to bat for you is just the beginning; his effort may fall short. Still, savvy, forceful advocacy offers its own rewards, not only to you but also to those you lobby. You will develop important new relationships, insights, and skills. An official may not be able to help you every time, but he will be a better public servant for having tried.

As you apply the lessons in this book, remember one basic tenet. In lobbying as in business, the only sure way to fail is to do nothing. The rest is a matter of practice, persistence, and patience.

INTRODUCTION

Getting Ready to Lobby

First, call upon all of those who you know will give you something; next, apply to those you are uncertain whether they will give or not; and finally those who you are sure will give nothing, for in some of these you may be mistaken.

—Ben Franklin

A shopper just told you that the city council is considering an ordinance to eliminate on-street parking in all downtown neighborhoods. While the change could hurt many businesses, it would devastate stores in the historic district, like yours. With inadequate public transportation and no nearby garage, your site would become inaccessible to many of your customers. In fact, you realize in dismay, the ordinance could force you—and many of your neighbors—to relocate.

Angry, you pick up the phone and call the first number listed on the city council Web site: "Resident Complaints." This turns out to be a general communications portal, offering multiple routing options for city departments you've never heard of. After several transfers among bored-sounding receptionists, you reach the office of the mayor—and another routing portal. By the time a polite young woman comes on the line, identifying herself as a mayoral aide, you are out of patience and demand to speak to her boss. She explains that the parking ordinance is an initiative of the city council president, not the mayor, and suggests you contact that official to voice your objections.

In utter frustration, you hang up and do no more—except complain to neighboring storeowners, reinforcing everyone's perception that small businesspeople are powerless to fight City Hall.

In fact, you could play a significant role in this situation. The city council president probably doesn't realize the severity of the parking shortage in the historic district. It is clearly not in the city's interests—or in hers—to force stores to relocate. But unless someone brings the problem to her attention, she can't fix it. Even the most diligent, business-friendly official can't have personal knowledge of issues in every neighborhood.

Like most other decision-makers, the council president relies on constituents for feedback. You could easily provide the pertinent information, perhaps backed up by calls from other storeowners. This intervention might well be enough to convince her to derail the ordinance in its current form, thus helping everyone: you, neighboring businesspeople, the city and the official herself. In the process, you would learn how it is possible to influence a far-reaching government decision—without paying a lobbyist.

WHAT LOBBYING MEANS TO YOU

If you've never done it, lobbying can seem a mysterious, intimidating process. That's partly because it has become a multimillion-dollar business, conducted largely behind closed doors. But long before there were paid professionals called lobbyists, ordinary people were exercising their constitutional right to influence decision-makers. "Congress shall make no law ... abridging ... the right of the people peaceably to assemble, and to petition the government for a redress of grievances," reads the First Amendment to the U.S. Constitution.

Of course, when Thomas Jefferson wrote those words, he could not have foreseen the complexity of modern government, or how extensively it would become intertwined with commerce. But precisely because of this evolution, contemporary lobbying has become more potent than in Jefferson's day—and far wider in scope.

The current legal and regulatory environment is a maze of overlapping federal, state, and municipal rules. Even the largest multinational corporations no longer confine their attention to Capitol Hill. However, big companies are still fairly insulated from the actions of local government. The size and diversity of their operations dilutes the impact of laws or regulations in any one state, county, or town.

But if you run a small or medium-size business, your profitability—often, your very existence—can be threatened by local decisions. A single change in the city zoning code can devalue your assets. One new county tax could drain your revenues. A poll conducted by the National Federation of Independent Business suggests that small employers understand these vulnerabilities: they contact state and local officials about legislation or regulation far more often than they reach out to Washington.[1]

For large companies, influencing state and local government is a smart management strategy. But for small ones, it is a survival skill. There is another key difference: when big corporations need the ear of officials, they hire lobbyists. Other businesspeople are on their own. This helps explain why only a fraction of small employers actively engage in lobbying.[2] They realize the importance of advocacy, but can't afford a professional and don't know—or are too intimidated to believe—that they can do it themselves.

Here is the good news: to lobby effectively, you do not need political power or an "inside track." Nor do you need a special degree or certification. But you do need to learn a disciplined, intelligent approach. That's what this book will teach you.

THE TARGET-TOOLS-TACTICS APPROACH

The Target-Tools-Tactics approach is based on a few simple principles.

1. In popular mythology, government officials are either arrogant politicians or bumbling bureaucrats. In fact, they are no different from any other occupational group—despite some bad apples, most are highly skilled at their jobs and genuinely dedicated to the public interest. Moreover, even the loftiest officials have a duty to be accessible and responsive to their constituents. No citizen should be put off by the trappings of power—big offices, gold domes, fancy titles—because that power ultimately resides with the public. There is no reason to be hesitant or timid about expressing your views or asking for help at any level of government. Cynics will always claim that only money talks in the halls of power. But research says otherwise: as recently as 2009, political scientists at Michigan State University found that grassroots lobbying "has a substantial influence on legislative voting behavior."[3]

2. As a businessperson, you know that different marketing tools are called for in different situations. In a price-sensitive market, you might need to focus on discounts. If your product is new, advertisements will be critical to get people's attention. For many expensive or complex items, a personal pitch is necessary to close the sale. In the same way, a variety of methods can be used to influence government; the key to success is choosing the right combination.

3. The advocacy marketplace is highly competitive. Not only are there people like you on both sides of almost every issue; as one advocate among many, you must compete just to get heard above the din of requests, demands, and opinions. Again, a marketing analogy: your message must be effectively positioned against the alternative, even (or especially) if the alternative is to do nothing. You must craft that message in accordance with your target's characteristics and mindset.

These principles give rise to the three building blocks of a successful lobbying effort:

1. Target: identifying, analyzing and connecting with the person or public body in the best position to help you.
2. Tools: selecting and mastering the communication device(s) most appropriate to the task.
3. Tactics: shaping a message that gets both attention and serious consideration.

But building blocks must rest on a solid foundation. That foundation is a basic understanding of how state and local governments work.

WHO DOES WHAT IN STATE AND LOCAL GOVERNMENTS

There are many in-depth sources of information about American government, both online and at any public library. An introductory list is provided in the Appendix. But the fundamental mechanisms are simple to understand and remember, especially since they are visible every day, to any citizen who takes notice. Review this background—it will help you make sense of your own state, county, and town.

State Government

All state governments share essentially the same structure, based on the federal model of a separation of powers. There are executive, legislative, and judicial branches, elected or appointed by independent processes and designed to check and balance each other.

The executive branch, headed by the governor, has the power to administer and fund the daily operations of government. Depending on the state, other key executives may include the lieutenant governor, attorney general, treasurer, and auditor. State departments and agencies—each with their own elected or appointed officials, sometimes both—are in charge of specialized areas, like transportation, housing, health, labor, and commerce.

The legislative branch of state government has the power to make laws and public policies. With the exception of Nebraska, all state legislatures are bicameral: citizens elect members of an upper house (the "senate") and a lower house (called a "house of representatives," "house of delegates," or "assembly"). A voting district may be represented by just one legislator, but some have more.

The judicial branch adjudicates disputes, both civil and criminal. A state's highest court also has the power of judicial review, meaning that it can invalidate laws found inconsistent with the state constitution.

Reflecting wide differences in demography, geography, and politics, each of the 50 states has distinct governance priorities. For example, a densely populated state is more concerned about preserving open space than a state with thousands of undeveloped acres. But all have roughly the same set of responsibilities. In general, state government either controls or has a major say in managing transportation corridors, natural resources and public lands, hospitals and public health facilities, public higher education, and aid to the needy. States regulate many business functions, like incorporation and employment, and set standards in areas like occupational safety and environmental stewardship. Of course, states also have the power to raise revenue through a wide variety of taxes.

Local Government: Municipalities and Counties

The distinguishing characteristic of local government is that it is fragmented and inconsistent. For starters, there are over 80,000 local jurisdictions across the U.S. But for the purposes of small business lobbying, two categories are most important: municipalities and counties.

Municipalities include cities, towns, townships, villages, and boroughs. Their governance structures are established by charter and incorporated by the state. Here are the three most common forms of municipal government:

1. A mayor and council
The mayor is the chief executive officer of the municipality; his powers may be defined in the charter as "strong" or "weak." A strong mayor can veto laws passed by the council, appoint most administrative officials, and control the budget. In general, a weak mayor needs the approval of the council to act. Councils are legislative bodies, which originate and vote on local laws. There can be as few as two council members,

or dozens. All are elected by the voters, either at large or from individual election districts called wards.

2. A council-manager system

In this form of government, the voters do not choose a CEO. Instead, they elect council members who in turn appoint a manager as chief administrator of the town. The council sets policy; the manager implements it (and in practice, often makes interpretations or modifications). While some councils select a "mayor" from amongst themselves, this position is largely ceremonial.

3. A commission system

Municipal commissions combine executive and legislative powers in one body. Each elected commissioner functions as the head of a city department or agency; collectively, the commissioners pass laws and set policy.

There are several variations on these basic shapes. One of the better-known is in New England, where executive authority rests with an elected "board of selectmen" while legislative power is exercised by citizens themselves in periodic "town meetings." Some rural communities also provide for grassroots decision-making.

But across all structures, municipalities deliver and finance the services and safeguards that citizens most depend on as the underpinnings of their quality of life. These include public safety, local transportation and traffic management, public education, sanitation and pollution control, local parks and recreation, and, of particular importance to small business, land use planning. Like states, municipalities have the power to impose a variety of fees and taxes. They often require local business registration and licensure.

County governments are essentially coordinating bodies. Though some have independent responsibilities—and almost all levy some form of property or sales taxes—most counties exist primarily to administer the services (and allocate the funds) of the state among a specific group of municipalities. Typically, counties are also repositories of birth, death, debt, election and property ownership records.

The number of counties per state ranges from a few to hundreds. The most common governance structure is a board of commissioners or supervisors that exercises both legislative and executive authority. In a minority of counties, there is also an elected CEO called a county executive or supervisor.

DECIDING WHERE TO BEGIN

How do you choose the right level of government for your lobbying effort? First, keep in mind that there might be more than one. If you want to fight sales taxes, for example, there are probably different assessments levied by your state, county, and town. Similarly, it can be challenging to pin down the origin of a specific employment, environmental, or public health regulation.

But you can, at least, eliminate a few dead ends and pick a promising direction for your efforts. Here are three guideposts:

1. Where your issue has the most concentrated impact.

Let's say a billboard near your store has been repeatedly defaced by graffiti. The location is on a major municipal thoroughfare. However, because the road is also a regional artery, it is under the jurisdiction of the state. Should you call your state legislator to stop the blight?

Probably not. While the graffiti could be noticed by any member of the traveling public, it will disproportionately bother local motorists. People who live, work, and shop in the immediate area will get the most concentrated exposure—and make the most frequent complaints. In all likelihood, then, this is a municipal issue. You should take it up with the mayor, town council, or police commissioner.

2. Where the money goes.

Most of the issues that motivate small business advocates center on money: taxes, fees, fines, and other charges imposed by government. But which government?

Consider who collects the revenue, and for what. Everyone knows that libraries charge fines to defray the cost of books. In the same way, states impose motor vehicle license fees to fund safety inspections. Towns sell building permits to pay for code enforcement.

The links aren't always so clear-cut, but a money trail will often lead to the right place—or at least the right vicinity.

3. What the documentation says.

Sometimes the most obvious clues are the ones you are least likely to notice. Check every document related to your issue: look for official stamps or seals as well as names, titles, and addresses. While these identifiers can be obscure—referring, for instance, to some independent commission or authority you never heard of—they will offer at least a starting point for your search.

MYTHS ABOUT LOBBYING

1. Lobbying is sleazy.

In recent years, the image of lobbying has been dirtied and distorted by those who have abused it. The public has come to see lobbyists—paid or not—as hucksters, panderers, and crooks whose stock in trade is bribes and payoffs.

To be sure, there have been (and still are) influence-seekers who are richly deserving of disdain. But there is nothing inherently sordid about lobbying, any more than there is about business itself. All interactions with government, just as with customers, can be carried out honorably—or not.

It is true that lobbying, like business, was once a free-for-all. But the days of brazen vote-buying are long gone. Today's lobbyists are heavily regulated and constantly scrutinized, from Capitol Hill to Town Hall.

Old caricatures die hard. But you shouldn't let them obscure your view of current realities—or of your own lobbying opportunities.

2. Lobbying is futile.

If poorly planned and sloppily executed, lobbying is, indeed, futile—just like any other slapdash activity. Look back at the opening vignette: it points out the difference between purposeless venting and a thoughtful effort to influence government.

It is important not to confuse futility with unpredictability. There are no guarantees in lobbying; no matter how persuasive your effort, it may be doomed by political forces and public opinions out of your control. You will find that in government, priorities—like people—can shift unexpectedly and dramatically.

But you will also learn that the vast majority of decision-makers are far more accessible and responsive than folk wisdom suggests. You can't win every argument. But you can, with a reasonable investment of time and energy, get heard and taken seriously. You can develop skills—and establish relationships—that will make lobbying easier every time you do it. When approaching an official, you shouldn't think of yourself as a supplicant; as a local businessperson, you are an anchor of the community who deserves a say in government.

3. Lobbying only works for big corporations.

Big corporations pay millions to professional lobbyists. But they also spend lavishly on other business activities, like advertising. That doesn't mean a small businessperson can't compete. It means that her marketing—like her lobbying—must be a highly personal, owner- or manager-driven effort.

It also means that she must pick her battles. Some national and international issues are so broad and complex that it is a full-time job to stay on top of them, let alone alter their outcome. In these situations—routine for large companies and organizations—professional lobbyists provide a valuable and necessary, albeit pricey service.

But if you run a small business, a decision at Town Hall can loom larger than a ruling in Washington. Your day-to-day operations are mightily affected by the actions of municipal, county, and state officials. Fortunately, these are the decision-makers you can lobby most convincingly on your own behalf—with the right preparation. That you are not a hired gun will only enhance your credibility and persuasiveness.

HOW TO USE THIS BOOK

This book is designed as both a manual and a reference. Here are some usage suggestions.

First, skim Chapters 1–3. Because each of the three building blocks (Target-Tools-Tactics) will be wobbly without the others, it is helpful to get an overview of what you will need to do before you begin any part of it.

Next, familiarize yourself with the models and samples in the Appendix. As you develop your own lobbying materials, you can return to these examples over and over for ideas, direction, and clarification.

When you are ready to think beyond mechanics to politics and ethics, read Chapter 4. To be an effective advocate over the long term, you must be alert to these broader dimensions of lobbying—and scrupulously honest when confronting the issues. Here you will also find guidance for seeking contracts from state and local government.

Even if your issue doesn't precisely match any of the scenarios in Chapter 5, take some time to review and reflect on these common applications of the Target-Tools-Tactics approach. They are designed to provide a sense of how the pieces fit together in any successful lobbying effort. This chapter will also acquaint you with some basic government terminology.

Scattered throughout the book are brief tips and exercises called "Try It." In "From the Trenches," you'll find real-world examples of business advocacy at work. Here are examples:

TRY IT

Many local governments create official or quasi-official boards of local businesspeople who volunteer to advise the governing body. Find out if your town has such a group—usually called an Economic Development Committee, Business Improvement Board, or the like—and ask if you can attend a meeting. The members will appreciate your interest, and they can be an excellent source of information, contacts, and advice.

FROM THE TRENCHES

Grassroots economic development groups are particularly helpful in small, tight-knit communities where every business counts.

For example, when officials in the rural town of Gardiner, New York (population 5,300) wanted to attract new investment, their first step was to organize a Business Improvement Committee. Its inaugural meeting drew a packed house of local residents and entrepreneurs.

"After just one meeting ideas are plentiful and prospects, perhaps surprisingly, seem bright," reported the local newspaper. One of the officials described the committee as " 'a process' to figure out what the town collectively, as a government, a business community and residents, could do to make existing businesses stronger and attract new business."[4]

Some sections end with a feature called "A Different Angle." In a question-and-answer format, this material offers additional perspectives and applications of what you have learned. For example:

A DIFFERENT ANGLE

Question:

A new city health inspector has slapped your nail salon with numerous "violations." Most relate to long-standing or trivial conditions never cited by his predecessor. When you point out this inconsistency, he responds that state law has gotten tougher since the last inspector was on the job.

Who is your target in this situation? Should you go to City Hall and challenge the judgment of this inexperienced sanitarian—or lobby your state legislator to change the law?
Answer:
You should do both. It is possible that this inspector is overzealous or incorrect. But if the law is unreasonable, the next inspector won't be any better.

Before you put the Target-Tools-Tactics approach into action, take a few cautionary steps:

1. Calm down.
You may be reading this book after trying—but failing—to influence government. Chances are, the experience wasn't happy—and neither were you.

But you need to put your anger aside. The goal of lobbying is to get results, not revenge. Give yourself enough time to refocus and recharge before you get started.

2. Be realistic.
In lobbying as in business, no one wins every time. Long-term success takes skill, but also patience and resilience.

3. Be optimistic.
In lobbying, optimism is infectious. It would be naive to suggest that a positive attitude alone will influence a decision-maker, but cynicism and negativism rarely help.

Finally, keep in mind that this book isn't only for businesspeople who lobby on their own. If you choose to advocate as part of a group, increasing your individual expertise will strengthen the collective effort.

RETURN TO CITY HALL

Now, revisit the parking ordinance scenario at the start of this Introduction. In light of what you have learned, how could you proceed more productively?

Target

The first step is to confirm who is sponsoring the parking ordinance (you should never trust secondhand information). Check the city Web site to see if the proposal is posted; otherwise, call the office of the mayor or chief administrator. When you locate it, download or request a copy of the text for future reference.

Assuming you verify that the city council president is the major backer, she is your target. You can now use the techniques in Chapter 1 to research her background and priorities.

Let's say you learn that she has made a career of looking out for pedestrians. Her record brims with projects like speed bumps and crosswalks. Now you understand why she proposed the ordinance. In her view, on-street parking is a safety hazard, not a business issue.

Tools

Your next task is to select one or more advocacy tools most appropriate to this situation. Perhaps you've heard from other business advocates that the city council president prefers in-person to written communication. Moreover, you want an opportunity to show her photographs and a video of current parking conditions. So, after an introductory email, you call her office to arrange a meeting.

Tactics

As a result of your research, you are able to put yourself in the shoes of your target, convey how it would help her to help you, and anticipate opposition. These are the key dimensions of framing, or shaping, a message.

Here are a few sample message elements:

1. Because of the narrow streets, numerous crosswalks, and strict speed control in the historic district, it is already the city's safest pedestrian shopping area. (You might obtain accident data from the police department to make this point.)

2. Eliminating on-street parking with no transportation alternatives will encourage many drop-offs and "stopping and standing" violations. These could actually increase, rather than decrease, accidents.

3. You are eager to organize the business community in support of her efforts to expand public transportation.

4. You are also willing to reach out to neighborhood groups to explain to concerned citizens why the parking ban is unnecessary and counterproductive.

There are many more scenarios and suggestions throughout the book. Now: you are ready to be your own lobbyist.

ONE

Target

In the fall of 2008, New Jersey legislators were deluged with pleas to support a set of tough new laws to stop "puppy mills." In droves, the emails poured in from veterinarians, dog groomers, and pet shop owners.

But despite this advocacy avalanche, not one New Jersey official took action. All the passionate messages were in vain. Why? The laws were before the legislature—in Pennsylvania.

Targeting missteps of this magnitude are uncommon, but smaller ones are not. Mayors routinely field complaints about state regulations; legislators get calls to fix sidewalks. Time is wasted, opportunities are lost, and tempers fray while the errors get sorted out.

The right lobbying target is as important as the right sales prospect. The same principle applies to both advocacy and sales: if you target everyone, you target no one. The time you must invest to effectively target officials and customers is similar, too. Good research can take weeks. But it is a low-risk, high-return investment. With it, your efforts will be focused and efficient; without it, they will be blurry and duplicative.

Targeting for advocacy is unique in one important way. While you can't approach a potential customer until you have a product to sell, you can—and should—develop relationships with lobbying targets before you need their help. In this chapter you will learn how.

Section 1: Target Research. What information do you need, and where can you find it? This section will discuss sources and research techniques.

Section 2: Building Relationships. Getting to know government decision-makers before you have a problem will be a big help when you do. Here you'll learn how to develop these and other helpful relationships.

Section 3: Coalitions. One way to heighten your visibility with a target is to form a coalition with others who share similar goals. This section describes two successful models and offers tips for coalition-building.

SECTION 1: TARGET RESEARCH

Where to Start—Official Web Sites

Begin by choosing the level of government most likely to handle the matter that concerns you. Then, on the appropriate Web site—municipal, county, or state—you can identify who is in charge of what. Except in the smallest towns, you will find links to every board, department, and agency. In those tiny jurisdictions, or if it's unclear exactly where your issue fits, you can email or call the office that handles matters in the same ballpark. Read the descriptions; scan "frequently asked questions." Your goal is to learn as much as possible about how the jurisdiction operates, and especially about the person or people calling the shots.

Sometimes a conversation or meeting with office staff is all it will take to solve your problem—say, a paperwork snafu or other routine foul-up. But for anything out of the ordinary, you will need the ear of an elected or appointed decision-maker. That's why most of your target research—like most of this book—will focus on these officials. Whatever your lobbying goal, their insight and influence can help.

This is true even when the official lacks direct authority to alter the policies or procedures affecting you. If you are denied a building permit by the planning commission, for example, the commission chair can't change the rules; land use decisions must conform to local, county, and state laws. But his advice can save you time and frustration when you resubmit your application. He can also tell you whom and how to lobby for better laws—he may dislike the current ones as much as you do!

Another common issue: you are cited by the board of health for a violation you believe you didn't commit. Again, the board must act in accordance with public health laws. But if there is any possibility that you were treated unfairly, it would be productive to meet with the mayor. While she, too, must respect the regulations, she can ask that the case be re-opened and reviewed in light of your concerns.

At the state level, indirect influence can be helpful if your business is affected by the rules of a department or agency. By determining how a law is implemented, these guidelines can turn a benign policy into a costly burden. For example, a new law may direct your state's health agency to strengthen its food safety monitoring program. That is a laudable goal. But it doesn't justify an agency plan to triple the frequency of restaurant inspections and the volume of paperwork required of restaurateurs.

Any restaurant owner could protest directly to the agency during the period allowed for public comment on new rules. But it would also be effective to contact legislators, who vote on the agency's annual budget. While lawmakers can't always block administrative decisions, they can communicate forcefully that the law was not intended to punish restaurants. At a minimum, their indirect involvement could ensure that other options get a second look.

So it is worth the time to cast your net widely at the start: the more decision-makers you research, the sharper your judgment will be when it's time to choose one (or more) as your lobbying target.

TRY IT

Another reliable resource for basic structural information is the League of Women Voters. This nonpartisan political organization specializes in voter education; to that end, many of its local, county, and state chapters compile a range of easy-to-understand government guides and directories. Some are online; others are available only in print versions. Most are free and can be obtained directly from the League (http://www.lwv.org) or through a public library.

More Online Resources

While there is enormous variation among local government Web sites, a patient researcher can usually unearth much more than just skeletal facts and job descriptions. It will take time, but you can compile a fairly revealing dossier on key decision-makers by digging into some or all of these five basic categories of information:

- Minutes and agendas of public meetings
- Budget documents
- Tax records
- Lists of vendors and public contracts
- Audits

As you review this material, patterns will take shape. You will see not just how officials vote, but what matters to them—in particular, how they spend money and to whom the money goes. It is also worth scrutinizing the minutes of public meetings. Here you'll find summaries of discussions, presentations, and debates.

A DIFFERENT ANGLE

Question:

What are the "shelf lives" of different kinds of information?

Answer:

There is no "expiration date" for information about your target's voting record. In fact, it can be eye-opening to track his behavior over time.

The duration of a public contract can vary from a few months to several years. You must check the terms of the original agreement to know if it is still in force.

If you are researching annual budgets, audits, or other financial records, keep in mind that the fiscal year of a public body may differ from the calendar year. For example, your town's fiscal year might run from July 1 to June 30.

A small number of local governments have yet to establish a meaningful online presence. If yours is among them, you can obtain the same key documents at Town Hall (there will probably be a copying fee) or, in most cases, at the public library.

A word of caution: in municipal budget documents, labels can be misleading. For example, an expenditure for "information management" can mean computer training in one town, but library supplies in another. A line item marked "general operations" could camouflage a slush fund. If a clear definition isn't provided, always request one.

FROM THE TRENCHES

Municipal budget entries can be not only obscure, but downright bizarre. In 2008, it was revealed that the New York City Council routinely appropriated millions of dollars to organizations that did not exist. As reported by the New York Times:

"The maneuver, in which funds were set aside for fictitious groups like the Coalition of Informed Individuals and Senior Citizens for Equality, allowed Council members to later spend the money on community programs they supported without obtaining the mayor's approval ... Since 2001, about $17.4 million was budgeted for dozens of fake community groups."[1]

The array of resources on state Web sites is, in general, both broader and deeper than on local sites. It is easy to find legislative rosters and to identify who sponsors what legislation. Voting records may be searchable by legislator, by subject, and by individual bill (proposed law). You can often find separate sites for the upper and lower house of the legislature, for political party caucuses, and for the executive branch of state government (the governor and other top administrative officials). If you are interested in the proceedings of a standing committee (these are topical, ranging from appropriations to veterans' affairs), check for archived Web casts.

State agencies and the judiciary will also have their own Web sites, with lists of officials and links to major programs and publications. Be sure to take advantage of search engines; state government is complicated both in structure and in terminology, and the information you want may turn up somewhere you didn't know to look.

FROM THE TRENCHES

Despite all the information that is readily accessible, a surprising amount still is not. In its 2008 study of transparency in government, the Massachusetts Public Interest Research Group found that fewer than half the states offer citizen-friendly, Google-type access to budget and public contract documents. Fortunately, the rest of the country is working to catch up to the new standard. The study concluded:

Legislation and executive orders around the country are lifting the electronic veil on where tax dollars go. At least 18 states currently mandate that citizens be able to access a searchable online database of government expenditures. These states have come to define "Transparency 2.0"—a new standard of comprehensive, one-stop, one-click budget accountability and accessibility.[2]

After you have combed official jurisdictional sites, search online newspaper archives to flesh out an official's bare-bones profile. Look for direct quotes as well as reportage of what she has stated, asked, criticized, and defended. A skilled journalist will be able to convey the official's temperament as well as her opinions.

FROM THE TRENCHES

While unusual, it is sometimes possible to find published reports that give real insight into the emotional or psychological state of a key decision-maker. This example portrays a mayor who is clearly feeling the stress of her job:

Three hours into a gathering of the Bainbridge Island City Council with no end in sight, Mayor Darlene Kordonowy broke down into tears . . . Her eyes red and voice shaking, Kordonowy said Bainbridge is a tough city to lead . . . The usually upbeat city leader . . . apologized for being "a tiny bit emotional," took a sip of water, folded her hands and led the group for another three-plus hours of work before the long and exhausting night ended.[3]

If you are researching an elected decision-maker, don't forget to read accounts of her most recent campaign. In addition, check the Web site of her political party. While you may need to sift through a lot of hyperbole, there are likely to be highlights from her history and accomplishments; these can offer a valuable window onto her priorities.

TRY IT

Depending on the kind of information you seek, it can be enlightening to peruse the records of political contributions received by an elected official. While reporting requirements and formats differ from state to state (and sometimes across jurisdictions in the same state), some basic list of campaign contributors should be accessible from the Division of Elections. From this list, you can learn whether the official gets financial support from other businesspeople, groups, or individuals with an interest in your issue.

Finally, you can hunt for comments about your target on the plethora of community, political, and self-appointed "government watchdog" blogs. But be cautious. For example, say your research leads to a councilwoman who wants to lower business taxes by cutting jobs at Town Hall. She sounds like your perfect target. But one blog slams her as a phony. Another derides her "poor management." What isn't clear is that the first critic is her campaign opponent, while the second blogger heads the public employee union. Obviously, neither is objective; it is up to you to make a balanced judgment.

Many blogs are blatantly partisan. Some habitually disguise political attacks as hard information. One dead giveaway that a blog is less than credible: any observation laced with threats or expletives.

TRY IT

While it is prudent to be wary of unfamiliar political blogs, some have proven to be fair, informed, and engaging. A good way to find the reputable ones: start with the staff blogs on the Web site of a traditional newspaper. Often, these will offer links to or mentions of other blogs that have been vetted by professional journalists.

Freedom of Information Requests

If you can't find the government information you want, don't give up. In most cases, as long as it exists, you have a right to it. Federal "freedom of information" laws (often dubbed "sunshine laws" or "open records laws" on the state level) mandate public access to the vast majority of public records. Taxpayers are entitled to know how their money is spent; government at every level must allow you to view (and usually to copy) most files, contracts, and agreements. But that doesn't mean it will be easy. Unfortunately, the process of making a records request, from the Statehouse to the tiniest town hall, can be tedious and costly.

For example, say the online city budget includes a line item for "computer maintenance." You want to know how much is being spent on laptops. Begin on the Web site by looking for a link called Right to Know, Freedom of Information, Public Records, or the like. There you will find any standard forms and instructions. (Alternatively, you can obtain the materials in person at City Hall.) The Appendix includes an example of these forms.

But the forms may not be readily accessible, or provide only cursory instructions. In that case you can write a letter, also modeled in the Appendix. Whatever your format, specificity is the key to success.

Overly broad requests are the most frequent cause of processing delays and unanticipated copying costs. The problem can develop all too easily, because a natural, conversational description of what you want is rarely the tightest. For example, if you simply ask for "laptop maintenance agreements," you could end up with reams of incomprehensible legal documents—but none of the billing information you're actually seeking. Alternatively, you might get voluminous but outdated contracts.

FROM THE TRENCHES

Occasionally, a freedom of information request triggers processing costs so exorbitant that the problem ends up in the courts. While unusual, this report from Bergen County, New Jersey offers a cautionary tale:

A North Jersey county clerk is allowed to charge a company more than $460,000 to block out Social Security numbers on 22 years of land transaction records, the state Supreme Court ruled . . . [The company] wanted microfilm copies of more than 2500 rolls of microfilm. Bergen County said it lacked the staff to comply with the request and . . . would have to hire a private company to convert the pages to print or another electronic format. . . .[4]

The task is tedious, but you need to pare down your request to its essentials. Be precise about dates; name any relevant individuals, firms, brands or products. If you require the information in a certain format, identify it.

When you file your request, ask when you can expect the information. Then follow up. Keep in mind that the law requires a reasonable response time. If you sense that someone is dragging his feet, write a letter to the top administrator in charge of public records—and be sure to copy other key officials.

TRY IT

Justifiably or not, the freedom of information process often turns contentious. Sometimes you will get more cooperation by starting with an informal, friendly request. Call or email the mayor (or other relevant official), and explain what you need. It can't hurt to try this first, and could actually produce faster results.

Offline Resources

Obviously, you will maximize your research efficiency online. But it is worth the extra time to get out from behind your computer. Even the best Internet resources cannot replace these:

1. Attending public meetings

No cyber-profile can fully capture an official's personality and demeanor—for instance, his sense of humor or what makes him angry. The best way to learn how a target behaves at a public meeting is to attend one (preferably more).

In the Appendix, you will find a list of tips for how to work a public meeting to make yourself visible. But you can learn a great deal as a passive observer. Look for triggers: for example, certain kinds of questions that clearly irk your target. During public comments, is he enthusiastic and engaged—or circumspect and wary? Do some topics spark his interest, while others consistently bore him? You will find these observations invaluable when the time comes for you to participate.

2. Talking to knowledgeable people

Whomever you target, you are not alone. Many others have interacted with him for all kinds of reasons, and you can learn from their experience. Put the word out on your professional and personal grapevines that you want input from other advocates. Check with your trade association. If you know anyone who works in government—even in a different branch—ask them for feedback. You can also try relevant public chat rooms.

3. Reading political mailers

Finally, a purpose for all that campaign literature that floods your mailbox before an election: it can give you useful insight into your target's worldview. Not all of these mailers are available online, but campaign staff will be happy to provide them. Don't hesitate to ask even long after the election—every political headquarters is crammed with boxes of unused material.

4. Watching public affairs programs on cable TV

Many public meetings are televised on local access channels (some are live, others recorded). If you can't attend in person, this is another way to watch your target in action.

Some cable channels also run candidates' debates, documentaries, and other public affairs programs oriented to the local community. These shows are not slick, but at their best, they can be thoughtful and enlightening.

Other Research Topics

While the major goal of your research is to identify and learn about a target, you shouldn't stop there. From the same resources, you can glean additional information that will make you a better lobbyist. Consider these topics:

1. Public opinion and the political climate

Lobbying, like governing, does not occur in a vacuum. Be sensitive to the outside influences on your target. For example, it is unwise to fight water-quality regulations right after an oil spill. You should avoid pushing any controversial proposal a few weeks before an election. Good timing won't guarantee the success of your effort—but bad timing can doom it.

FROM THE TRENCHES

Officials will appreciate your sensitivity to timing, because they must consider it too. For example, New York's Nassau County chose to launch a new efficiency initiative just as the local economy collapsed, dubbing it a New Deal for Nassau.

Taking a page from The Great Depression's playbook, Nassau County . . . unveiled its "New Deal for Nassau," a program designed to boost government efficiency by cutting down on delays caused by bureaucracy and red tape . . . [to] stimulate the economy and attract new companies, development and jobs.

"This is the time to get this done," [legislator] David Mejias said. "Because the economic climate is the way it is, people will be willing to try anything."[5]

---

2. The history of your issue

Just as every official has a past, every issue has one, too. Learn from others' mistakes. Look for strategies that (almost) worked. Identify previous supporters and opponents.

3. The details of your issue

Often the small print in a law or regulation looms larger than you think in determining how it will actually apply to your business. Before speaking out or taking action, bone up on the administrative nitty-gritty to avert mistakes that can be costly, embarrassing, or even illegal.

FROM THE TRENCHES

When a state sales tax increased from 5 to 6.25%, some Massachusetts retailers advertised their intention to temporarily pay the tab themselves instead of passing it along to their customers. While the gesture seemed a harmless and consumer-friendly form of passive resistance, it turned out to be illegal.

The state Department of Revenue informed the startled sellers that they were in violation of a little-noticed provision in the statute: "It is unlawful for any vendor to advertise or hold out or state to the public or any customer, directly or indirectly, that the tax or any part therefore will be assumed or absorbed by the vendor."

A legislator who was attempting to change the provision described the situation as "a lose-lose for [both] consumers and retailers."[6]

4. Public meeting procedures

Lobbying often includes speaking, or testifying, before a government body. To do it well—indeed, to do it at all—you must research procedures for public comment. Every meeting has its own rules, but at a minimum you should expect restrictions on when you can speak, for how long, and on what topics. You will find examples of these public comment rules in the Appendix.

TRY IT

If you plan to address a hot topic, likely to bring out many speakers, ask if the rules permit advance sign-up. Or arrive before the start of the meeting to nab an early slot.

5. The public building layout

Getting lost at the Statehouse can cost you a chance to testify. Going to the wrong office at City Hall can cause delays and mix-ups.

The layout of many public buildings—especially historic structures—is illogical. Signage can be poor. Parking is often nonexistent. Don't assume it will be easy to find your way around—in fact, you should assume the opposite.

A DIFFERENT ANGLE

Question:

   You want information about the record of a county commissioner, but her only past government experience was in another state. How does this affect your research?

Answer:

   Local government terms and titles can vary widely. So you'll need to learn the other state's language before asking questions or looking for documents. Also, be alert to differences in the forms and rules pertaining to freedom of information requests.

Summary: Dos and Don'ts for Target Research

Do:

- Dig beneath the surface of official Web sites.
- Use media archives, political literature and blogs
- Broaden your perspective by exploring public opinion and the history of your issue.

Don't:

- Limit your research to just one potential target.
- Underestimate what you can learn by attending public meetings.
- Hesitate to make a Freedom of Information request.

SECTION 2: BUILDING RELATIONSHIPS

   Few small businesspeople make an effort to interact with—or even meet—state or local government decision-makers until they have a problem. Then, especially if the matter is urgent, they're forced to scramble. Why the lack of bridge-building? There are two major reasons: one is real, one is perceptual.

   Time, of course, is the real barrier. Relationships can't be forged on the fly. Proactive business advocates make a costly commitment—at least several hours each month, often more. But if your business is heavily regulated or otherwise dependent on government (and few are not), the absence of relationships can be costlier. When the inevitable issue arises, you'll find it hard to open doors—or even to know which doors to knock on. Without relationships, you are guaranteed to encounter a stranger instead of a friendly face.

No one needs an extra management burden. But every businessperson needs to look ahead. Getting to know state and local officials now means they'll be easier to find, talk to, and influence later.

FROM THE TRENCHES

When interviewed about what it took to lobby successfully, a group of small business advocates in New York were candid about how much time they devoted to their efforts. But they also stressed the importance of lobbying to long-term profitability.

Lou Basso, president of a human resources firm, attended 126 meetings with state legislators over the course of a decade. He finally got what he wanted: upgraded standards for his industry.

Bob Cutrona, head of a building maintenance company, convinced lawmakers to eliminate a state sales tax—at the cost of spending "more than a third of his work week" on related activities.

After eight years of advocacy, environmental consultant Jennifer Carey became so visible in the state capitol that she won appointment to the influential New York State Small Business Advisory Board. " 'I realized that [each business] has a silent partner: the government,' says Ms. Carey . . . 'I feel I'm playing some part in the democratic process. And you do see progress—but it can take a long time.' "[7]

The other major barrier to relationship-building is a perception that it is hard. If you've never talked to government officials, you may expect to find them aloof or pompous.

In fact, the vast majority are gregarious and friendly. Keep in mind that skillful interaction with the public is part of their job. Never feel that you are imposing on an official's time; by reaching out, you are actually helping him understand what is on his constituents' minds. It is in his own interest to put you at ease and to be attentive to your input.

You can get to know officials in two ways: by going to them, or by inviting them to come to you. The ideal is to combine both approaches.

TRY IT

Do you know the names of your mayor and other municipal or county officials? If not, don't be embarrassed. But do fill in this gap in your local knowledge—if only so you'll know who they are in case you meet any of them informally around town.

Going to Them

For the purpose of getting to know an official, attending government meetings has limited value. While useful for watching how she performs her job, it is a poor way to make a personal connection. Instead, go back to your research to determine the kinds of community gatherings your target is likely to attend. Many will be free of charge; but a dinner or other function where you can spend time with your target could be worth the price of a ticket. Here are a few ideas:

- Does your target sit on the board of a charitable organization or institution? If so, she will surely attend its fundraisers and programs.
- Is she aligned with citizen activists, like environmentalists? Perhaps you could join her at a park cleanup or Earth Day event.
- Does she have a pet project, like a municipal sports league? Look for opportunities to be a sponsor or participant.

Of course, you can choose to get involved with your target's political party or election campaign. This is a valuable option, but it carries some risk; for this reason, it is discussed separately in Chapter Four.

Many local governments are proactive in reaching out to the business community. For example, your county might run an economic development seminar or a jobs fair. Be sure to attend such an event even if the topic doesn't exactly match your interests. It is still an excellent opportunity to interact with officials—and to get a jump on new initiatives.

FROM THE TRENCHES

The Economic Summit in Maplewood, New Jersey is a typical example of a municipal outreach event, attracting about 75 small businesspeople and officials.

"Mayor Vic DeLuca kicked off the two-hour event . . . listing seven things Maplewood Township will do, or already has done, to help strengthen the local business community," said a newspaper report. "It has implemented a 'buy local' campaign, compiled a list of local food establishments . . . posted all bids online to facilitate local business'[s] access, and waived the $100 fee to have an outdoor café. . . . "

Not all the attendees went away satisfied, according to the story. However, each got the chance to start a dialogue with the mayor and his staff—the first step toward an ongoing relationship.[8]

Inviting Them to Come to You

If you've never done it, you may be surprised to learn how easy it can be to get your target to come to you. As long as you can deliver an audience, most public officials will gladly accept your invitation to give a speech, serve on a panel, or otherwise participate in a business-focused forum. An informal event is fine, too; for example, you could host a "meet and greet" for the mayor to talk casually with home-based business owners in your neighborhood. Call or email his staff scheduler to make the arrangements (but first, nail down the specifics of time, place, and format).

One caveat: it is challenging to get a commitment from the governor or other top policymakers. But it is not impossible. Just be persistent, and try to be flexible in case of last-minute changes in her schedule.

TRY IT

Your invitation will be especially attractive if you are working with a group that can offer the official an award or citation for his service to the business community. (Caution: read about gift restrictions in Chapter Four. You can recognize the official's achievements without giving him a costly trinket.)

A DIFFERENT ANGLE

Question:

Is it appropriate to invite more than one official to participate in the same event?

Answer:

That depends on your format. A panel discussion, for instance, would be an excellent way to involve multiple officials at the same time. You might also schedule one guest at the start of your program, and another at the end. No one will be insulted as long as each invitee is informed in advance that he or she will be sharing the spotlight.

Relationships with Staff

Decision-makers are the most influential people in government, but they are by no means the only ones who matter. In many situations, rank-and-file staff determine who gets access and what gets processed first—or last.

Most of these much-maligned bureaucrats are dedicated and highly knowledgeable. Like you, they take pride in their work and appreciate when it is acknowledged. Whenever appropriate, ask their opinions. Pay close attention to their advice. Work on building relationships; in a public office, no currency is more valuable than the trust of key staff.

Here are a few ways to earn that trust:

- Be helpful. If your research would simplify their work, share it. If you have identified a new information source, suggest it.
- Be visible. Keep your staff appointments. As often as possible, provide material and ask questions in person. Introduce yourself to everyone in the office.
- Be respectful. Too many citizens treat the average public servant with disdain. This is a silly—and shortsighted—mistake. Staff are gatekeepers as well as facilitators. They can be important allies.

A DIFFERENT ANGLE

Question:

According to the municipal Web site, your mayor maintains weekly office hours at City Hall for citizens with "unresolved issues." At the moment, you have no "unresolved issues." Can you show up just to introduce yourself?

Answer:

While the mayor is making a special effort to reach out to people with problems, that doesn't mean he will turn away other constituents. Anytime a public servant is in a public place for a purpose related to his job, it is perfectly acceptable to approach him for informal conversation—or for any other reason. (However, you should make an appointment if requested.)

Summary: Dos and Don'ts for Building Relationships

Do:

- Get to know officials when you don't need their help with a specific problem.
- Take advantage of opportunities for informal interaction.
- Respect and cultivate relationships with staff.

Don't:

- Kid yourself—building relationships takes time.
- Think you are imposing on an official by talking informally with him.
- Be intimidated.

SECTION 3: COALITIONS

Another type of relationship-building can also boost your lobbying effort: forming a coalition with others whose goals complement yours.

Many small businesspeople belong to trade associations and state or regional commerce groups. These organizations already offer advocacy, visibility, and professional development, among other benefits well worth the cost of membership. So why create another one?

Sometimes, only a local, tightly focused group can tackle problems like land use conflicts or regulatory disputes that affect only one town or county. In other situations, a new coalition may spring up spontaneously, as an offshoot of loosely coordinated action among like-minded colleagues, neighbors, or friends.

This was the genesis of Vest Pocket, a coalition in Salt Lake City, Utah. Its members are small businesspeople with a big ambition: to remake relationships between the commercial community and local government.

The Vest Pocket Model

In 1995, the owner of a small Mexican market in the city painted a mural on the side of his store. The artwork helped draw the attention of passersby. But it also caught the eye of local officials, who fined him for violating the building code—then removed the meters that allowed his customers to park outside. At the same time, the inspectors ignored a mural displayed on a Starbucks just up the street.

When word of the disparity got out to other local businesspeople, several decided to rally around the beleaguered merchant. The group—including owners of a bike shop, bookstore, pet clinic and specialty grocer—protested to the planning commission and city council. Members also met with the mayor. Their lobbying effort succeeded—not only in getting the fine rescinded and the parking meters replaced, but also in launching a citywide small business coalition.

Today the Vest Pocket Coalition has 350 members. It has stayed true to its roots, frequently mediating between businesses and local government or neighborhood groups. But Vest Pocket's leaders define its mission as largely proactive. "Relationship-building is key," says president Ellen Reddick. "No one victory is enough to build a strong small business community; we need ongoing conversations with city and county government officials and with civic groups. We educate our members to be vigilant about local issues and, if they can, to head off conflict."

Some disagreements, however, are inevitable in a city with many new businesses in established residential neighborhoods. When they get involved, Vest Pocket mediators try to take an incremental approach, breaking down large problems into small, more manageable ones.

For example, Reddick observes, restaurant operations often raise the hackles of residents as well as regulators. "A lot of the problem is unfamiliar sounds, smells, and activities. Instead of taking on everything at once, we work through the issues one at a time." Sometimes, a minor change—like redirecting a venting hood—can resolve a major dispute. When local officials are cooperative rather than confrontational, they can readily address simple but contentious matters like trash pickup.

Vest Pocket's biggest challenge is to educate members and keep them up to date when everyone faces time and economic pressures. One approach is to bring the organization to them; as a supplement to meetings in a central location, Vest Pocket representatives offer localized "area training" to businesses in a small area, sometimes block by block. There are also evening seminars, online training, daylong retreats, and other activities.

The educational programs explain key laws and regulations and demystify the workings of local government. "This is especially important for business owners who are just starting out; many are intimidated and confused," comments Reddick. "They don't know the system—what questions to ask or where to go for help." In fact, Vest Pocket often recruits members from among new businesses faced with zoning or regulatory problems.

Importantly, members are also encouraged to respect the broader community and to be good neighbors. Coalition leaders practice what they preach: Reddick and others are active with regional chambers of commerce, sit on local and state boards, and maintain ongoing dialogue with Salt Lake City and County officials.

Since it began with a fight on behalf of one small store, Vest Pocket has changed the face of a large and diverse business community. The challenges keep coming—but so do the victories. A recent highlight: the story of Mini Cupcakes.

In 2008, recalls coalition vice president Robin Carbaugh, the little cupcake bakery was started by a young woman "who did what she thought were all the right things; she checked all the right boxes on every city document." But two weeks before she was scheduled to open, an official turned up at her door to inform her that she was not in compliance with one of the regulations for a commercial bakery. To operate legally, he insisted, she must pay for a grease trap in a manhole in the street. The price tag: $40,000.

The distraught young baker had no idea what to do until Vest Pocket stepped in. It wasn't easy; the effort took research, site visits, and multiple meetings with the inspector as well as his boss. But in the end, the city relented. Mini Cupcakes was permitted to place a grease trap in its own kitchen, accessible for monitoring by the city. It was an example of what lobbying can accomplish—and its role as a fundamental business skill.

FROM THE TRENCHES

While much of their work takes place behind the scenes, Vest Pocket representatives don't hesitate to speak out when governing bodies, like the Salt Lake City Council, consider measures that could harm its members. For example, when the mayor suggested increasing business license fees to plug a hole in the city budget, coalition vice president Mary Corporon slammed the proposal. "If you're asking me if honestly $30 here or $15 there is going to put a business under? No it's not," Corporon says. "But I can also guarantee there is some business owner out there for whom this will be the final 'Why should I keep trying' moment. . . . " Corporon says that instead, the city should be nurturing business in order to increase its sales tax revenue and avoid future budget crises."[9]

The members of a coalition must share some common purpose. But a business-friendly group need not be limited to—or even initiated by—businesspeople. While the Vest Pocket model has been highly effective, coalitions also form around issues that matter equally to local companies, residents, and civic groups. The Lincroft Village Green Association is one of these.

The Lincroft Village Green Association Model

It started as a handful of neighbors worried about the fate of a single piece of property. Today, the Lincroft Village Green Association is a coalition representing over 900 members with a broad focus on issues of traffic, safety, access and road design. The group has become a resource for citizens, an advocate for local businesses, and a force to be reckoned with at Town Hall.

Lincroft is a small, historic, village-like section of Middletown Township, one of New Jersey's largest suburban municipalities. When LVGA formed in 1999, decades of rapid growth had already consumed almost all of the area's original farms. The community was left with increased traffic, decreased pedestrian safety, and one large parcel of undeveloped land.

The tipping point came when neighbors learned that the land, owned by a county college, was about to be sold to a large bank. The founders of what would become LVGA launched a petition drive opposing the sale. "We collected thousands of signatures in just a week and a half," recalls Mary Ellen Hintz, the first co-president. "People understood we had reached a crossroad that would ultimately determine the direction, success, and future character of our community. The time had come to speak up for our vision of Lincroft."

The group pleaded their case to Middletown officials, who ultimately arranged a land swap with the college and transformed the endangered parcel into a park. The early victory transformed LVGA, too. "It gave people hope," says Hintz. "Most were still wary of local government, but this outcome proved that at least some of the decision-makers would listen to citizens and were open to different points of view."

At first, only a few businesses showed interest in the fledgling organization. But there was a marked change when LVGA took on the major road issues that were costing them clients. "Some of these businesspeople had a lot of past experience with local officials, but their interactions had been sporadic and adversarial. They were frustrated and cynical because they weren't getting results," explains Roger Foss, another early co-president. LVGA was able to convince an array of storeowners, landlords, and professionals that working in isolation was no longer an effective approach. The businesses began to see a close connection between their long-term interests and the health of the surrounding community—a primary source of Lincroft's customers, tenants, and employees.

Like the residents, businesses were hamstrung by problems with road access, safety, and walkability. For example, when stores sought permits to expand parking or driveways, they were denied, in part, because of traffic hazards. Poor conditions for both pedestrians and bikers alienated senior citizens, young people, and other formerly loyal shoppers. As soon as commercial stakeholders were on board with their efforts, LVGA was ready to represent a broad cross-section of Lincroft in attacking these issues.

But it quickly became apparent that few coalition members were comfortable communicating with government: "Everyone absolutely dreaded it," recalls Hintz. So they started slowly, requesting volunteers to simply attend and observe public meetings. Over time, the LVGA representatives developed a sense of who was most influential on road issues. Then members like Hintz and Foss arranged a series of personal meetings.

By 2001, the progress they had made at Town Hall emboldened them to reach further. They lobbied the county officials who controlled regional routes, presenting data that showed correlations among road design, sales taxes, and property values. Using donations from members, LVGA hired consultants to critique projects long on the books. Their persistence paid off: in one case, the county set aside its own road-widening plan in favor of a roundabout option developed by the group. Officials were also convinced to abandon a long-touted "divided highway" concept that small stores feared as an impediment to their customers.

As the organization gradually built visibility and trust, its leaders were invited by county and town officials to participate in long-range road planning. Word spread around the region that LVGA had solid information and knew which officials to approach. A Lincroft Village Task Force was formed by Middletown Township to facilitate ongoing, face-to-face communication. But there were ongoing challenges.

"Our biggest challenge was the frequent turnover in government," says Hintz. "Every election meant a change in decision-makers. We were constantly selling ourselves to new officeholders, as well as reeducating our own members about who was in charge and what was going on."

Open community meetings became an increasingly important tool. "We held public meetings to share our knowledge and to recruit new supporters, and sometimes hundreds would show up," explains Foss.

It has taken 10 years of hard work, but today LVGA is widely perceived as a key community voice. Officials, residents, and business owners alike look to the group to comment on local issues, advocate for local interests—and get results. "The importance of working together has become self-evident," says Foss. "Now there are businesspeople who will put down their tools and even close their stores in order to attend one of our meetings. They can measure our value in terms of dollars and cents."

FROM THE TRENCHES

Even after a decade of success, LVGA is careful to frame its efforts as collaborative rather than adversarial. In a *New York Times* profile of Lincroft—which highlighted the coalition as a local powerhouse—Mary Ellen Hintz commented, "We don't come to meetings saying we are entitled. . . . When we want upgrades to the park, we raise the money. And when we want traffic calming measures, we do our research, which helps the government to make better decisions."[10]

Forming a Coalition

Some coalitions evolve naturally out of informal short-term alliances. For instance, several business owners who helped you start a petition drive could decide that it is in everyone's interest to continue sticking together. At the other end of the spectrum, you might need to put considerable thought and effort into recruitment. Another common scenario: there is a core of self-selected members, but you want to expand the group. Whatever the specific situation, a coalition builder can benefit by following these guidelines:

1. Define your issue as broadly as possible.

Perhaps you want to change your town's zoning code to permit more home-based businesses. Of course, you are focused on restrictions in your own neighborhood. But why not push for a study that could lead to community-wide loosening of the rules? You would pick up support from all over town—and have a shot at getting other helpful code adjustments, too.

FROM THE TRENCHES

Professional yoga instructors in New York City, who make an art of self-reliance, might seem unlikely coalition builders. But when the industry was targeted for possible state licensure, this highly diverse community—normally resistant to any hint of conformity—quickly coalesced around a broad but unifying goal: independence from government regulation.

The teachers formed a coalition and enlisted a state senator, Eric T. Schneiderman of Manhattan, to take up their cause, hoping that New York would buck the national trend. "It's really kind of historic in the yoga community," [co-founder] Brette Popper said.

Within days, [a representative of] the State Education Department said in an interview that the department would suspend the licensing effort . . . and instead lobby for legislation adding yoga to a list of activities that are exempt from regulation.[11]

---

2. Identify existing business or civic groups with goals that could complement yours.

Let's say you want streetlights illuminated later into the evening so downtown stores can extend their business hours. You could enlist the help of groups that have little interest in commerce, but strong commitments to promoting pedestrian safety or fighting street crime.

As another example, many small businesses lobby state and local governments to post contracts online. The goal of these companies is to become more competitive in the public marketplace. But expanding online disclosure also furthers the general aims of government transparency and accountability. Those aspects of the issue could attract watchdog and taxpayer organizations to your coalition.

A note of caution: the broader your coalition, the more important it becomes to formally obtain permission from all key participants before using their names in public statements that purport to represent the group as a whole. Establish reliable channels of communication to make sure everyone is included.

3. Identify your opponents.

There are two reasons to try to determine up front who is likely to oppose your effort. First, it will help you prepare to fight back. Second, it could lead you to some motivated, albeit unlikely, allies. The politician's old adage, "The enemy of my enemy is my friend," is equally durable among advocates. If you know who is working against your interests, that person's rival could be eager to help you.

4. Ask each of your coalition members to reach out to others.

Even in a small town, people move in different circles and have their own spheres of influence. By including each member in active recruitment, you will increase everyone's personal involvement with the coalition while building its numbers.

Keeping Your Coalition Alive

Many informal groups view themselves as temporary from the outset, and simply disband after achieving the goal that brought them together. But if you hope to sustain and build a coalition over time, you will need to focus on these key dimensions:

1. Education

No matter what or who originally brought the members together, issues, circumstances, and people change. A long-term coalition must keep members up to date and help them hone their advocacy skills. Training and education can be offered either on- or offline; Vest Pocket, for example, does both. Particular mechanisms and venues can be chosen for the convenience of members, and topics will be specific to your needs. What matters most is this basic reality: when it comes time to present a knowledgeable, persuasive front to government decision-makers, a coalition is only as strong as its weakest spokesperson.

2. Motivation

Like a business venture, an advocacy coalition will lose its edge unless leaders (and a critical mass of members) stay energetic and focused. But long-term lobbying inevitably brings demoralizing setbacks and defeats. Moreover, it takes patient, incremental spadework—with little immediate payback—to lay the foundation for major victories. How do you keep people motivated in the face of these realities?

Managing expectations is one important strategy: everyone needs to understand that advocacy is a marathon, not a sprint. Another approach is to divide big goals into more manageable, readily achievable ones. Whenever doable, this is a potent way to reinforce the value of the coalition as a whole while boosting the confidence of individual members.

Let's say your coalition aims to create a self-taxing municipal business improvement district (BID). Because BIDs cannot form without the approval of local government, your major goal is to secure the mayor's support. However, he has been unenthusiastic about these projects in the past, so you anticipate a protracted battle.

In the meantime, smaller-scale ancillary tasks could be tackled by coalition members. One example: since BIDs are typically self-managed by the local business community, there is a need to recruit volunteers for a potential BID board. This shouldn't be hard; many businesspeople would feel flattered to be asked. Other assignments with a high likelihood of success could include reaching out to civic groups or arranging public meetings and media interviews.

3. Visibility

By itself, a high profile in the community will not guarantee your coalition's success. But a lack of visibility can cripple your efforts.

Remember: the lobbying marketplace is noisy and crowded. From the humblest town hall to the grandest statehouse, you will always be competing with a babel of other voices and pressures. Here are three ways to break through the clutter:

- Attend—and be vocal—at public meetings.
- Sponsor, host, and/or help promote major community events (such as fairs and holiday celebrations).
- Build a media presence (as discussed in Chapter Three).

A DIFFERENT ANGLE

Question:

You have formed a coalition of businesspeople to lobby for insurance reform. It is a popular issue across the state. So you are not surprised when a candidate for the state senate—who is also a businessperson—expresses interest in being a spokesperson for the group. Knowing that he is an accomplished speaker, is there any reason to discourage him?

Answer:

First, get the opinions of other coalition members. But you should ask him frankly about his intentions: if he were to make partisan statements about the group or use it as a political platform, you could have a problem. Perhaps you could suggest that he take on this role immediately after the election.

Summary: Dos and Don'ts for Coalitions

Do:

- Define your goals as broadly as possible.
- Involve all members in recruitment.
- Identify both allies and opponents.

Don't:

- Think that only businesspeople can be effective participants.
- Overlook the need for ongoing education, motivation, and visibility.
- Leave any coalition member out.

Now that you know your target, it's time to choose the tools most likely to get—and keep—his attention.

TWO

Tools

No banker would give you a loan just because you sent an email telling him you want the money. On the other hand, why waste your time—and his—in a lengthy personal meeting if all you need to do is cash a check?

A variety of tools are available and accessible to every aspiring advocate. With practice, you can wield them with as much skill as a professional lobbyist. In this chapter, you will learn how to use each major tool—and what mistakes to watch out for when you use them.

Certain tools will be more or less practical and appropriate depending on how much time you can devote to your lobbying effort and on the nature of your issue or request. To help you make the best choice, tools are divided into two main categories and identified as Quick Fixes, Modest Investments or Major Projects. For each, you'll find an estimated time commitment and recommended applications.

Section 1: Tools for Written Communication. This section will compare email to postal mail, explain how to prepare testimony for a public hearing, and describe statutory and marketing petitions.

Section 2: Alternative (Non-Written) Communication Tools. Turn to this section for advice on making the most of a phone call, enhancing the value of a personal meeting, and deciding whether to stage a rally or community meeting.

Section 3: Tools to Avoid. In lobbying, as in business, anger and frustration can lead to poor choices. This section warns about lobbying techniques more likely to harm than help you.

SECTION 1: TOOLS FOR WRITTEN COMMUNICATION

Quick Fixes: Email, Postal Mail

Time Commitment: 1–4 hours
Best suited for:

- weighing in on an issue that affects many businesses
- making an initial contact to be followed up with other tools

Modest Investment: Testimony for a Public Meeting

Time Commitment: 4–12 hours to research and write testimony, plus travel and meeting time
Best suited for:

- influencing an action, most often a vote, that involves multiple decision-makers
- communicating facts, examples, and detailed information too lengthy or complex for a single letter
- putting your case, in your words, on the public record

Major Project: Petitions

Time Commitment: 6–12 months for a statutory petition, 4–8 weeks for a marketing petition
Best suited for:

- placing a measure on the ballot (initiative, referendum, or nonbinding question)
- getting others involved with your effort while documenting support for it

It takes time, energy, and sometimes extensive research to write persuasive letters, emails, testimony or petitions. There are faster and easier ways to communicate with decision-makers. But in most cases, none of the alternatives are equally effective. In lobbying, the most forceful voices almost always speak from a page.

Of course, you may sometimes face time pressures or other problems that preclude any contact beyond a quick phone call. In certain circumstances, a personal meeting can add a critical dimension to your case. But whenever possible, other techniques should be viewed as supplements to—not substitutes for—written communication. The reason is simple: written words have staying power. They can be stored, shared, excerpted, analyzed, and otherwise put to use in ways that other forms of communication cannot.

For example, you may spend an hour in a one-on-one meeting with a state legislator, making what you think is a powerful case for a new law. But when he talks to his colleagues, all your passion gets reduced to "a proposal from a constituent." That doesn't mean the legislator was unimpressed—in fact, he may be eager to work with you. But you gave him little or nothing that he can refer to, quote from, or build on. At any given time, he is juggling a vast array of issues and responsibilities; the details of one constituent meeting won't stick in his mind unless you cement them in a letter, memorandum, or other written format.

Another important reason to put your case in writing: an opponent may misrepresent it. For instance, at a hearing on your permit to create office space in a historic building, a neighbor could object on the grounds that you promised the town council you would never change the structure. That objection is easily overcome if you can quote from your actual testimony to the council, in which you committed to "respect the history of the building"—you did not pledge to avoid any alteration.

If you need some extra motivation to start writing, remember that one document can serve multiple lobbying purposes. Once you've composed a persuasive letter to a targeted official, you can also submit it to newspapers and blogs, share it with others in your business, distribute it to clients and vendors, and adapt it to create a fact sheet for meetings or testimony for public hearings. Excerpts from the letter might be appropriate on your Web site, or even in advertisements. For example, if you've lobbied the mayor for more parks, your sports-goods customers would probably be pleased to read about it.

As with any business skill, you will get better and faster at writing for advocacy the more you do it. The models in the Appendix will help you begin.

Email

While all forms of written communication share the advantages of permanency and adaptability, they differ on other dimensions. In particular, email and postal mail are often seen as interchangeable, but that's a mistake: each has distinctive strengths and weaknesses.

Obviously, emails maximize the speed of communication and the ease of replication. Because they are generally less formal than traditional letters, emails may also be quicker (or at least less intimidating) to write. In fact, you may not need to compose one at all; especially if you are addressing a state issue, the Web sites of many business advocacy groups offer standardized emails that you can deliver to a long list of powerful people with just a few clicks.

But the same characteristics that make email easy and fast can also undermine its persuasiveness. Take that cyber-form letter you sent from a Web site: if it originated with a well-known organization, you can assume that every decision-maker received hundreds, possibly thousands, of the identical communication. The recipients won't ignore it—on the contrary, their staff will carefully count the total number that hit the inbox. If your goal was simply to weigh in on an issue that affects many other businesspeople, helping to boost the number of missives supporting or opposing that issue may be sufficient.

But it is unlikely that the staff, let alone the decision-maker, will do more than glance at the actual text of standardized e-advocacy. Even if you have spent time adapting or personalizing it, as most Web sites allow, the chances are miniscule that anyone will notice. Moreover, while many diligent officials make a good-faith effort to respond to every constituent, the majority will not even attempt a reply to a cyber-blitz.

This is not to warn you away from email. But if you need to make a particular request or convey specific information—and if it is important to get a reply—you must compose an original e-message. Write with the same care and attention to detail you would apply when preparing any other business document. The relative informality of email can create a temptation to skimp on research, to be imprecise, or to ignore rules of grammar. Don't be tempted: think about how your email will read (and look) when downloaded. Stay away from odd fonts, confusing graphics, irrelevant illustrations and excessive use of italics or capital letters. Ask yourself: when distributed together with other high-quality lobbying materials, will my composition hold its own—or will it come across as sloppy and amateurish?

TRY IT

Writing an original email or letter takes effort, but you need not start from scratch. In addition to the general models in the Appendix of this book, you can also get ideas by browsing suggested advocacy messages on Web sites like the U.S. Chamber of Commerce Small Business Nation (click on "Take Action"). Challenge yourself to put a few of these standardized communications into your own words. This is the best kind of practice, even if the available text doesn't address your specific problem or issue.

Also, keep in mind that no one expects (or will be impressed by) flowery, elegant language. Just keep it simple, straightforward, and as brief as possible.

A DIFFERENT ANGLE

Question:
 Can you lobby via Twitter or Facebook?
Answer:
 Social media are not yet in general usage for lobbying purposes. That doesn't mean you can't try them. But ask your target or her staff first; for reasons of confidentiality and clarity, not everyone is comfortable using these tools.
 Also, if you use text messaging, be sparing with cryptic abbreviations. Your target might not take the time to decipher what "u" mean.

Postal Mail

As commerce itself has increasingly shifted online, postal mail has declined in advocacy use, especially on the local level. The average mayor who once received 50 constituent letters each week might now be surprised to see 10. Concomitantly, form letters have also begun to dry up.

While it might seem counterintuitive, this change has made traditional letters more, not less, valuable as lobbying tools. When relatively few people take the time to address an envelope, those who do automatically stand out. Of course, the same cautions apply to postal mail as to email: a form letter will get minimal attention, and your prose must be clear and clean. Long-winded, unfocused, poorly structured paragraphs will not be improved by a stamp.

But a well-written personal letter—especially when it conveys knowledge and passion—commands respect, and almost always gets a response. It may not be the response you want, but you will have an open door for more communication. Also, if you need to supplement your basic message with extra materials, your best shot at getting those materials noticed is to mail hard copies (with a letter of transmittal/explanation); email attachments are too easily overlooked, ignored, and deleted.

What types of supplements will most likely add value to your letter? Consider these:

– Tables, charts, or other quantitative analyses
– Graphs or other visual displays of data
– Photographs
– Maps or property surveys

It is critical to cite sources of all data. The most respected sources are institutions or organizations known for being reliable, nonpartisan, and unbiased, such as universities or government agencies uninvolved with your case. If you paid an expert to gather data, or found it yourself, there is no need to hide its origins—just disclose, as fully as possible, how and by whom the information was collected.

Don't rely too much on public opinion polls, which are popular but overrated as supplements to advocacy letters. That's because officials know that many polls lack scientific validity. With increasing frequency, "polls" are conducted by talk radio or television news hosts who invite their listeners/viewers to call a special number or email their views. This approach can amass a considerable number of responses; but the participants are not representative of the general public, only of the audience of that particular show.

TRY IT

If a particularly compelling public opinion poll comes your way, don't feel you must reject it out of hand. Just be sure to scrutinize the methodology behind it. Keep in mind that not every poll measures what it purports to measure; learn as much as you can about the sponsor of the research, and who was asked what questions.

In one study of how people respond to surveys, researchers asked participants what they thought of the federal Metallic Metals Act. The majority claimed to be familiar with the Act, and answered a series of questions about its impact, how it could be improved, and so on.

But there is no such thing as the Metallic Metals Act. These researchers showed that many people will respond to polls even when the questions are meaningless. Don't fall into the trap of relying on—or vouching for—such non-information.

You should never mail original documents or anything that must be returned. Also, certain supplements are a waste of time and postage. These include:

- Videos, CDs, or DVDs
- Books or pamphlets longer than a few pages
- Any material in a language other than English (unless you are sure the official or a staff member can translate)

You may be able to interest a decision-maker in one or more of these materials during a personal meeting or at a future date, but if you mail them as part of an introductory package they will almost certainly disappear into some file, ignored—if not into the trash.

One more cautionary note: when lobbying via postal mail, refrain from using return receipt, restricted delivery, certification, or other services that encumber the recipient. Unless you are mailing legal documents that must arrive at a specific time or be accepted by a specific individual, these services serve no purpose and will simply frustrate the office staff.

Finally, stay away from decorative inks, fancy papers, and extravagant packaging. They won't help—and could hurt if perceived as unprofessional.

The Five Biggest Email and Postal Mail Mistakes

Whether you choose to click or to stamp, steer clear of these common errors. They seem small but can have outsize costs in goodwill and respect.

Mistake #1: Misspelling the Decision-Maker's Name and/or Misstating His Title

There are officials who apply a simple rule of thumb: if the writer can't be bothered to address them correctly, his letter will go to the bottom of the pile, unread. Make it a habit to check this information on the Web or over the phone.

Misidentifying gender is a frequent faux pas, almost guaranteed to give offense. If it is difficult to determine whether your target is a woman or a man, don't guess: use their (correct) title without "Mr." or "Ms.," as in "Dear Mayor Jones" or "Honorable Judge Smith." Titles, like names, are readily accessible either on the Web site of the appropriate jurisdiction (town, county, state, public agency, etc.), or through the search engines of state and national business organizations, like the U.S. Chamber of Commerce or the National Federation of Independent Business.

Mistake #2: Using Unsubstantiated or Outdated Information

Your research need not be worthy of a doctoral dissertation, but you must ensure veracity. Provide sources for all data, and if you are not an expert, be up front about it. The decision-maker wants to know that you are truthful and conscientious, not that you can fill up a page with someone else's statistics.

Mistake #3: Forgetting—or Deliberately Omitting—Your Contact Information, Particularly a Home Address

There are three reasons to be sure you include your name, phone, postal address, and email address:

- First, you will not get a response if the recipient must hunt for you.
- Second, the official will want to know if you are a constituent (established by zip code and/or postal address).
- Third, most public offices have a policy of ignoring anonymous communications.

Mistake #4: Asking Recipients to Call You for Material "Too Sensitive" to Put in Writing

They won't. Officials have no time to play guessing games. Be clear about exactly what you have; if the information is proprietary or otherwise protected, check that you have a legal right to share it.

On the flip side of the coin, assume that anything you send to a public official will end up in the public domain. Your advocacy letter should not include information that could damage your business or harm others. If you feel compelled to share such material, make a specific request for confidentiality.

Mistake #5: Using Inflammatory Language, Insults, or Threats

This is always counterproductive. You cannot scare an official into helping you.

Testimony

Testimony is the narrative you prepare to read, or "testify," at a public hearing or meeting. It should do double duty, serving both as a speech and as a background document. Like testimony in a court of law, it becomes part of the official record of the proceedings. As such, it will be accessible to the media as well as to your supporters and opponents.

Public speaking is an art in itself. But polished oratorical skills are unnecessary to testify effectively: when your arguments are clear and persuasive, you need only read them audibly and with conviction.

The next chapter discusses specific message elements that are the foundation for compelling, memorable testimony. But in general, when testifying you should:

- Identify yourself and your company. (Unless your business is well known, you may want to describe what you do and cite your professional credentials, if relevant.)
- State precisely what you are supporting and/or opposing. For example, you may support a recycling requirement but object to the fee.
- Be long on facts and short on rhetoric. If you believe a new assessment will drive stores out of town, don't just call it a "store killer"—cite the actual number of enterprises likely to be hurt.
- Provide specific examples. How will the proposed change in parking regulations affect your customers?
- Make your points in order of their importance to you; assume they won't all be read and/or remembered.
- Respect time limits, which are usually in the range of 3–5 minutes. If your testimony is too long, it's fine to read a summary of key points, but be sure to bring enough copies of the full narrative to distribute to every member of the public body (and to the media, if you hope for press coverage).
- Offer to respond to the officials' questions. If you don't know an answer, pledge to get it and follow up.
- Leave enough business cards for every official.
- Say thank you.

The Three Biggest Myths About Testifying at a Public Hearing

Because few people do it routinely (unless they are paid lobbyists), testifying at a public hearing may be an unsettling prospect. It shouldn't be.

As long as your testimony is well prepared, you can be just as persuasive as any professional.

Myth #1: You Are Expected to Be an Expert

Unless you identify yourself to the officials as some type of consultant or scholar, no one expects you to be anything other than what you are—a businessperson concerned about the impact of their actions on your business. Moreover, you *are* an expert on your own business. Government decision-makers must deal with a dizzying array of issues every day, and they will welcome your testimony as an educational tool and a reality check.

Myth #2: The Officials Won't Pay Attention to Anything You Say

On the contrary, officials appreciate it when an ordinary businessperson comes to testify on his own time and his own dime. If anything, the fact that you are not a professional lobbyist is likely to get you more attention, not less.

Myth #3: You Are Likely to Be Attacked by an Opponent

Public meetings adhere to rigid rules of order and decorum. While you may have vociferous opponents in the audience, the presiding officer will cut them off if they are abusive or try to circumvent proper procedure, like speaking order or time limits.

It is possible that one or more of the officials will be hostile to your position and take the opportunity to challenge your remarks. But as long as you are prepared to back up your assertions, the interchange is likely to be civil, impersonal, and brief.

Moreover, regardless of who voices opposition during the hearing, you can benefit from listening closely to their arguments. In your next lobbying encounter, you will be ready to refute them head-on.

Sometimes, people get emotional or angry while testifying. That's understandable—if your business is threatened, it's only human to lash out at the source of the threat. But you should make every effort to come across as reasonable and polite, rather than bellicose or nasty. Try not to be disdainful or disparaging toward anyone. In lobbying, today's enemy can become tomorrow's friend. Moreover, especially on a local level, many officials who hear your testimony will readily offer to meet with you, visit your site, extend deadlines, or make other good-faith efforts to resolve your problem. It's simply bad business to alienate them.

TRY IT

Even if you're upset and frustrated when you write your testimony, you can keep your feelings out of the narrative. Here are examples.

Instead of saying something like this:	Try this:
"This proposal is crazy."	"I believe you were missing some key information when you suggested this."
"You must want to destroy my business."	"If you deny the permit, I will be forced to eliminate jobs."
"Anyone who supports this plan is stupid."	"I'm sure you want to hear from both sides."

Petitions

At its heart, a petition is simply a request—when stated forcefully, a demand—for action by some authority, backed up by the signatures of many individuals who want it. The authority may be a court of law: for instance, a party to a legal action may "petition" the judge for some decision or form of relief. But advocacy petitions are usually targeted to a specific public official, governing body, or administrative agency.

There are two basic types of petitions. One type is a statutory mechanism, used to set into motion the process for placing a ballot measure before the voters of a town, city, county, or state. The second type is solely a marketing device, intended to attract publicity, build enthusiasm, and demonstrate support. Both are powerful lobbying tools.

Statutory Petitions

In 24 states, citizens have the power to place a proposed new law (an "initiative") and/or a proposal to repeal an existing law (a "referendum") on the ballot for a statewide vote. This power, or some form of it, is also widely available in municipalities and counties—even where it is not allowed on the state level, as in New Jersey or Texas.

A petition for access to the ballot, either locally or statewide, must follow strict rules that vary by jurisdiction and type of proposition. The most common requirement is a minimum number of signatures, obtained from residents of the jurisdiction during a specified time. Sometimes, signature-gathering is restricted to designated sites. This task can be daunting, especially in a state or major city; for example, at least 50,000 people must sign a petition for a municipal initiative in the city of New York, while 20,000 signatures are required in Austin, Dallas, or Houston.

So it is not a casual undertaking—but petitioning for an initiative or referendum can force significant change that would not otherwise happen. For example, it took statewide citizen petitions to prohibit new assessments on the sale or purchase of real estate in Arizona, and to bar the government from taking private property for private uses in Oregon.

In many local jurisdictions, citizens may also petition for a vote on "nonbinding" questions or resolutions. In themselves, these ballot measures cannot change laws. But by expressing the sentiment of the community they can be extremely effective in getting the attention of officials and, sometimes, embarrassing them into casting the vote or taking the action petitioners want.

FROM THE TRENCHES

In Missouri, petitions are key weapons in an ongoing battle over eminent domain, the power of government to take private property for public use. Fulton businessman Ron Calzone heads Citizens for Property Rights, a group of eminent domain opponents which seeks a vote on placing new restrictions in the state constitution.

In 2008, Calzone's organization collected 428,000 signatures across Missouri. But according to the rules, the number was insufficient in one election district.

CPR is trying again, and its leader remains optimistic. "We fell short . . . by just a few thousand last year," Calzone said. "We are trying to start earlier this time, whereas last year we only had a few months to collect the signatures."

According to news reports, Missouri city officials are vigorously defending their eminent domain rights. But Calzone is confident: "Time is our friend . . . we just need enough time to get in front of enough Missourians."[1]

From Portland, Oregon to Portland, Maine, local petition drives are often spearheaded by small businesspeople with strong convictions and deep community roots. From zoning to taxes, they address many of the issues critical to success on Main Street.

TRY IT

If you are considering this route, you will need to obtain the rules and regulations of your municipality, county, or state. These are available from the board of elections or designated election official.

To get a general feel for what can be involved, you may want to browse two easy-to-follow online information packets. The City Council of Columbus, Ohio offers a one-page overview called "Initiative Petitions and Referendum Information." A much more extensive discussion is available on Portland, Oregon's Web site in its downloadable "City Initiative Petition Information Packet."

Petitions as a Marketing Device

A petition need not be aimed at the ballot to get attention, encourage word of mouth, and generate excitement. As a marketing device, it publicizes your cause by giving others a stake in it.

When you are unconstrained by statutory requirements, you can direct the petition to any authority you choose and ask for any action you want. Structurally, it must contain only three elements: a heading (like "A Petition to the Mayor of Hometown"); a statement of purpose/request (such as "We the undersigned request an expansion of free parking hours on Main Street"); and lined spaces for each person's signature, contact information, and home address. Look in the Appendix for an example.

However, because your goal is to appeal to the widest possible audience, you should write the petition with a question in mind: Why does this matter to anyone but me? The benefits of some requests, like a tax reduction, will be self-evident, but the reasons for others will need to be spelled out.

For example, you may be petitioning the town council to allow larger commercial signs on major thoroughfares. How will this help other businesses, or average shoppers? First, specify the problem: an unsightly proliferation of little signs with hard-to-read information. Point by point, you should then list every potential benefit, such as improved visibility; reduced clutter; and heightened awareness of local enterprise. If you believe the change must be made ahead of the holiday season, or by some specific date, say so.

While there will be no official number of required signatures, you should set your own goal and a realistic timetable for achieving it. One approach is to aim for a large absolute number. But if you live in a small town or will be circulating the petition among a relatively small group, like downtown retailers, a large percentage of the affected population—say, 75 percent—may be more impressive.

There are many ways to collect signatures. You will probably want to make the petition available in your place of business and bring it to the attention of employees, customers, and vendors. It can be emailed to user groups, posted on chat boards, and linked to Web sites. Clipboard-toting petitioners are a familiar sight at community gatherings, like fairs and school events. Often you can generate interest outside supermarkets and sports or entertainment venues. However, you should not begin before checking with local officials and storeowners, as it is common to require petition permits in public places, as well as some form of written permission to solicit on private property.

A DIFFERENT ANGLE

Question:

Several people with experience in circulating petitions have encouraged you to hire professional signature-gatherers. Is this a good idea?

Answer:

Paying for signatures will almost certainly yield a bigger number than you could collect on your own. But you can end up with pages of illegible names. Worse, the signatures could be exposed as forged or phony.

If you choose to go this route, take two precautions. First, pay only for verifiable signatures. Second, take it upon yourself or trusted allies to periodically observe the circulator at work; this will put him on notice that you care about his methods.

Once you have met your signature-gathering goal, how should you submit the petition? That depends on your target and on the nature of your request.

A petition may always be hand-delivered to any member of a public body, or their staff, at a regularly scheduled meeting of that body—whether it is welcome or not. At other times, or to reach an administrative agency, you can bring it to the staff office and ask that it be routed to the appropriate official. (Be sure to get the name of the person who accepts the petition.) Mailing the petition is risky, as it can easily get damaged or lost. If there is no alternative—say, it must reach a distant state capitol—send the original but keep copies of every page.

If your request is at least partly intended to influence public opinion, it should also be submitted to the media (more in the next chapter on how to get press attention).

Whatever method you choose, try to let the signatories know when and to whom the petition was delivered. Whether you post the information on a Web site, set up a phone chain, or generate a story in the local media, this step is important for two reasons. First, it is only fair—every person who signed the petition became your partner in this effort. Second, you need to keep them engaged for possible follow-up. For example, if there is no response to the petition, you may put the word out that people should call or email the targeted official. If you decide to speak on the topic at a public meeting, some of your supporters would probably want to attend.

FROM THE TRENCHES

When officials in Berkeley, California put forward a controversial proposal to construct a public plaza, they were confronted with a petition circulated by the managers of a local business.

"The city of Berkeley has not shown the capacity to maintain its open public spaces," said John Coleman, the bookkeeper of Earthly Goods, a women's clothing store in the area.

When the plan was defeated, the credit went to those who initiated the neighborhood pushback. "We care about the community, but we have to be realistic about what it takes to run a business," Coleman said.[2]

Summary: Dos and Don'ts for Written Communication

Do:

- Double-check names and titles.
- Provide sources for all data.
- Be concrete and specific.
- Research relevant requirements, such as time limits or number of signatures.

Don't:

- Rely on a standardized message if you want an individual response.
- Attach superfluous materials.
- Overuse rhetoric.
- Be sloppy or discourteous in any written communication.

SECTION 2: ALTERNATIVE (NON-WRITTEN) COMMUNICATION TOOLS

Quick Fixes: Phone Calls

Time Commitment: 20 minutes to prepare a script, 60 seconds for the call
Best suited for:

- registering a "yes" or "no" position on an issue
- arranging a personal meeting
- offering help

Modest Investments: Personal Meetings

Time Commitment: 2–4 hours, including preparation (extra time could be needed for in-depth research or to develop detailed materials)
Best suited for:

- humanizing an issue by telling your story face-to-face
- using props or visual aids to make your point

Major Project: Holding a Rally or Community Meeting

Time Commitment: 1–4 weeks to lay the groundwork, 3–5 hours to set up and run the meeting
Best suited for:

- raising the profile of your issue
- bringing attention to who is supporting you

You can't wait for a response to a letter if your problem is an emergency. Nor can you count on delivering testimony if the key vote is scheduled for this afternoon. In these situations and others, it is impractical to rely on written tools. More generally, alternative lobbying techniques can lend dimension, human interest, and even drama to your effort.

Phone Calls

Phones ring all day—and long after hours—in many government offices. Calls like yours are expected and routine. That's why they have limited persuasiveness. Most of the time, unless you have a specific phone appointment with the decision-maker, you will only be able to talk to staff or to a machine. Your message may or may not be relayed quickly and accurately, and some of its immediacy and interest will almost certainly get lost in the translation.

However, even a single call is far better than nothing. At a minimum, it can get your name added to a list of people who want to be counted for or against an issue or action. Numbers of calls on a particular topic matter, even if the substance gets lost.

A call is the easiest way to arrange an appointment, request information, or confirm the arrival of a letter or other advocacy document. If you are calling for help, ask to be connected to the staff person who specializes in solving problems like yours.

Like any other lobbying tool, the phone should not be used without forethought. Unless it is just a scheduling call or a simple question, you should write down the key points you hope to make—or ideally, prepare a script—before dialing. A model telephone script is included in the Appendix.

Whatever the reason for your call, start by identifying yourself and providing contact information. In a government office, a call from a "friend" or "source" will be dismissed.

If you must leave a message, simply state the issue you are calling about and (briefly) give the reasons why you support or oppose it. If you have a problem and need a return call, indicate the nature of the problem (Sidewalk repair? Garbage pickup? Tax dispute?) and when it's best for someone to reach you. Don't bother leaving a lengthy, detailed, passionate voicemail message; no one can take the time to transcribe it, and you will be asked to repeat all the information (and probably put it in writing) anyway.

When you reach a staff person, make your case in a minute or two, specify the action you hope the official will take or what you want him to look into, and offer to answer any questions. Don't hang up without identifying next steps; it is especially important to clarify who is responsible for what. Is there a document you must mail to the office? Will a staff person get answers for you? Can you expect a call from the scheduler who arranges personal appointments? Even if you are not asked to do so, it is a good idea to record your understanding of the conversation and send a summary email. Include the name of the person you spoke to or expect to hear from.

Unless there is an emergency, be patient. If a week goes by, feel free to call back. For a variety of reasons—a key official is out of town, another office is closed, records are difficult to locate—there may be a significant delay in responding to you. It's fine to be persistent, but you won't speed things up by being belligerent. If you're truly at the end of your rope or believe that someone is irresponsible or incompetent, you can come to the office in person or call a higher-level official. If you have reason to suspect dishonesty, immediately contact law enforcement authorities (or call the whistleblower hotline, if one is provided in your community).

For one important purpose, the telephone is underestimated and underused. Make a personal call to any official who has been particularly helpful; it takes just a few moments to say thank you. Because she is probably overwhelmed with problems and criticism, your thoughtfulness will be appreciated—and remembered.

Let's say you have a friendly relationship with an official in another town or branch of government. Should you ask him to call the appropriate decision-maker on your behalf?

Unless they are sworn enemies, it probably can't hurt. But be realistic about jurisdictional boundaries. A mayor's call won't solve a state contract problem; a state legislator has no power in a municipal land use dispute. Beyond the limits of his office, the most your friend can do is put in a good word for you, or perhaps expedite a response.

Also, keep in mind that the judicial system is largely a world unto itself. Only rarely is it helpful—or ethical—for a legislative, executive, or administrative official to intercede in any matter before the court. Usually, the wisest course for all concerned is to avoid discussing it.

A DIFFERENT ANGLE

Question:

Should you call a target at home or on his personal cell number?

Answer:

Usually, his preferred contact number will be posted on the jurisdiction's Web site (or staff will be authorized to provide it over the phone). The appropriateness of using another number depends on how you obtained it.

If a number appears in any public directory, he probably expects some constituents to use it. However, you will be starting off on the wrong foot if you call a number given to you by a third party, who may have broken a promise of confidentiality.

As a general rule, it is advisable to stick with official lines of communication unless you have a real emergency. If you do try a personal (or private business) number, be courteous: avoid calling late at night, leaving multiple messages, or discussing your issue with an employee or a member of his family.

Personal Meetings

Meeting face-to-face with a decision-maker can add substantial value to your lobbying effort, especially if the visit is timed to follow up on a letter or other recent contact. Personal meetings are particularly important, even vital, when:

- The decision-maker must touch, smell, taste, or otherwise handle something in order to understand or evaluate your case. Perhaps you need to demonstrate the clarity of a water sample or compare the size of merchandise.
- You are highly skilled in personal sales or believe you are most persuasive when making eye-to-eye contact.
- The decision-maker has been unresponsive to emails or letters.
- Others who have lobbied this decision-maker report that he prefers personal to written communication.
- You do not want a written record of your conversation.

Under certain circumstances, however, personal meetings can be unwise—even prejudicial. Most importantly, if you are engaged in litigation with a public body, you should never seek or participate in a personal meeting with a member or representative of that body. What seems a trivial conversation or harmless encounter can come back to haunt your court case.

At a political function, like a campaign rally or fundraiser, you should feel free to interact with your target—but refrain from the temptation to pull her aside for an impromptu "meeting." Politics and government can be a toxic mix: for both ethical and legal reasons, it is in your best interests to keep them separate.

Also, timing matters. Hold off on the meeting if:

- You're not sure you've identified the right target. It's pointless to meet with the zoning board chairman on a matter in the purview of the environmental commission.

- Your facts are incomplete.
- The decision-maker has asked you to wait until after a specific vote, hearing, or other development that is relevant to your problem.
- You are too angry or overwrought to discuss the situation calmly.

What if you are offered an immediate appointment with staff, in lieu of a future meeting with the official? Don't reject it out of hand: many legislative offices have staff who specialize in handling certain issues or serving particular constituent groups. It's possible that your problem could be solved in the time it would take to arrange a later meeting.

Also, it is a mistake to dismiss the opinions of key staff. Ultimately, you may need or prefer to lobby the official directly, but a favorable staff report will smooth your path.

Sometimes it is a good idea to bring another person to the meeting, particularly if that person is more conversant with the issue than you and better able to respond to questions. Your story may be more dramatic or memorable if related by a colleague, employee, client, or neighbor. When appropriate, an articulate child can be an extraordinarily effective presenter.

You should also consider bringing props, even if you can make your point without them. Visual aids are especially useful, like a PowerPoint presentation (preferably on your own laptop), photographs, maps, or charts. Check in advance on the availability of any special equipment or setup you may need. If you have a petition with many signatures, this is an excellent time to display it.

In advance of your meeting, prepare a plan and checklist for yourself and an agenda for all participants. Most important, bring a fact sheet or other summary document to leave with the decision-maker. You will find models in the Appendix.

Meeting Time-Wasters and Turnoffs

A personal meeting with a busy official is a significant lobbying opportunity. Do not compromise your effectiveness or squander valuable time by:

- Name–dropping.
  Even if you have dozens of influential friends, naming them won't impress (or intimidate) a public official. It will just make you seem arrogant. The only exception: if another official has approved or endorsed your request, it is appropriate to say so.

- Showing off your knowledge of local politics.

  No matter how much you think you know, your target is virtually certain to know much more. By trying to sound sophisticated, you could unwittingly come across as naïve.

  More importantly, a lobbying meeting is about government, not politics. Your political opinions or allegiances are—or should be—irrelevant.

- Being unprepared.

  It is better to reschedule the meeting than to muddle through with incomplete or inaccurate information.

- Being late.

  Get directions to the site in advance, if you need them. Should you be delayed by circumstances beyond your control, call as soon as you can. (In this case, do not rely on email; you can't be sure how frequently the inbox is checked.)

- Being overly familiar, jocular, flirtatious, or otherwise disrespectful.

  This applies both to the official and to every member of her staff.

- Threatening, bullying, or being deliberately confrontational.

  In particular, do not interrupt to dispute the official's every point.

- Bringing more people than necessary.

  You accomplish nothing by simply filling up chairs. (In fact, there may not be enough chairs!) Be sure that every person you invite to the meeting can and will make a contribution.

- Using silly gimmicks.

  It is almost never helpful to wear a costume, sing a song, hand out candy, or otherwise risk embarrassing yourself and your business.

TRY IT

Would you make a sales pitch to a major client without rehearsing it? Your lobbying meeting deserves just as much advance preparation and attention to detail. Run through your presentation from start to finish at least once with someone who is up on the issue. Make sure there are no glitches in your PowerPoint presentation, problems with any props, or errors in your written material.

A DIFFERENT ANGLE

Question:

You have tried for months to arrange a meeting with a state official, who repeatedly puts you off or cancels appointments at the last minute. What should you do?

Answer:

Every public servant has an obligation to be accessible to constituents. You should complain (in writing) to this official's superiors. If he holds elective office, consider a letter to the editor of the local newspaper or to a popular political blog; voters should know about his lack of responsiveness.

Holding a Rally or Community Meeting

You don't need the skills of an event planner to bring advocates (or potential advocates) together. Assuming your problem is widespread or your issue motivating to others, all you need is a location, some time to devote to publicity, and a short but action-oriented program. While it takes effort to pull together, a rally or community meeting can be a highly effective supplement to other lobbying tools. Even if used alone, it sends a message to decision-makers that you are focused, energetic, and serious about your cause.

Of course, an official can be impressed by your rally only if he knows about it. Media coverage is important; in the next chapter you'll learn what reporters are likely to write about. But with online postings, flyers, and word of mouth, you can generate a great deal of buzz on your own—especially in a small town or among a specialized group like restaurateurs or dentists. You can also use the event to kick off a long-term, high-profile effort, like a petition drive or the formation of a new community group.

You can stage the meeting in your own place of business if it is large enough. But if your space (or parking) is limited, consider a local library or community center. Some large institutions, like hospitals or colleges, will host a public event if it is complementary to their mission.

An effective program may be as brief as an hour, as long as it includes three elements. First, you must introduce yourself and reiterate the purpose of the meeting. Although most attendees will know why they came, some may have brought guests who aren't sure. Circulate a sign-in sheet to get everyone's name and contact information.

Second, you should introduce any public officials or recognizable community leaders in attendance. Assuming they came to support your cause, thank them and ask if they wish to say a few words. It will be motivating to the audience to see early commitment from influential people; when the news gets out, it will also help persuade other leaders to get on board.

End with a call to action. What, exactly, do you want supporters to do? When? Tasks could include writing an email or letter, attending a hearing, signing a petition, or simply spreading the word among colleagues and friends. Whatever you request, be sure to explain its significance to the overall effort. Also, announce your plans for any additional meetings; if another gathering is unnecessary, offer to keep people apprised of developments via phone calls or email.

TRY IT

If you're not sure that your cause would attract many others to a rally or community meeting, it's better to test-market the idea than to risk an embarrassingly small turnout. Contact business associates, customers, and friends; post on blogs and chat boards; advertise in free local newsletters or on community Web sites. Ask people for an advance commitment to attend a gathering at a specific day and time. While they won't all show up, more than 20 early commitments suggests you've tapped into a widespread concern; fewer than 10 means you're probably on your own.

A DIFFERENT ANGLE

Question:

How should you handle an opponent who shows up at your meeting to argue against your goal, especially if he is discourteous?

Answer:

Generally, the most effective way to shut down an opponent (without further inflaming him) is to allow him to have his say, respond briefly to his arguments, and then ignore him. If he becomes seriously disruptive—say, by heckling the speakers—you are justified in asking him to leave. In the most extreme case, you can threaten to call the police.

Summary: Dos and Don'ts for Non-Written Communication

Do:

- Use, in most cases, as supplements to written tools.
- Maximize the personal touch.
- Research, review, and rehearse.

Don't:

- Be repetitive or long-winded.
- Get impatient or accusatory.
- Be dismissive or discourteous to staff.

SECTION 3: TOOLS TO AVOID

You can get an official's attention by stalking her, picketing her home, defacing her property, or hacking into her computer. You can also get arrested. No matter how serious or frustrating your problem, don't allow anger to cloud your judgment. If there is the slightest chance that an action is illegal, don't even think about it.

Also beware of so-called guerrilla marketing tactics, which seek to "ambush" consumers with unconventional selling messages in unexpected places (for example, by tattooing ads on bald heads). As adapted to lobbying, these methods generally rely on shock value and over-the-top provocation.

FROM THE TRENCHES

The mayor of Hoboken, New Jersey was furious when a sarcastic billboard went up in front of a major transit hub. The sign, mounted by a local realtor, sought to stoke public anger about the town's recent financial trouble—or at least take advantage of it.

"Cut your Hoboken property taxes 47%. We'll help you leave," read the highly visible message.

But if the billboard was intended to influence Hoboken's tax policy, it failed. "This is totally inappropriate and we are demanding the sign be taken down," said [Mayor] Dave Roberts.[3]

You may get short-term results from stunts like heckling or hunger strikes, but at the cost of your target's long-term animosity. As in business, a reputation tarnished by offensive, outlandish behavior is difficult—in some circles, nearly impossible—to restore.

Whatever tool you choose, it can be only as persuasive as your message. The next chapter will explain why some messages get results—while others get ignored.

THREE

Message Tactics

The visitor in your office is a pleasant, knowledgeable saleswoman. She has come to pitch a new brand of software. You are open-minded—there is no competing product, as yet—but unsure why you should make an immediate commitment. If you wait, the price might drop. So you ask her: what's the rush?

"It's really important to act now," she responds, "because if you buy today, I'll get a big bonus!"

Needless to say, you close your checkbook.

There is no such thing as "independent" communication. Every message begins with a source (the advocate), who gives it shape and heft before it gets delivered to a recipient (the decision-maker). Whether or not a message is persuasive depends on that shaping.

When you are developing and delivering a message yourself, you can control every facet of it. Part I takes this approach.

In Part II, you will learn how to work with the media and word of mouth. These are higher-risk venues because they can't be controlled, but you can learn the skills of managing them.

Part I: The Message You Control

Section 1: Message Framing. The shaping process is known as message framing. To do it well takes considerable thought and practice, like any other business skill. But in the same way, framing pays off. It helps ensure that every part of your advocacy message advances your position; no point is counterproductive, ignored, or wasted. This section explains the tactics of framing.

Section 2: Message Comprehension. For your message to be persuasive, it must be understood. This section suggests ways to enhance comprehension.

Section 3: The Messenger. A well-framed message can be undermined by the wrong messenger. Read this section for advice on who is likely to make an effective spokesperson—and who is not.

Section 4: Message Structure and Tone. In this section, you will learn how the substance of a message can be affected by its structure and tone.

Part II: The Message You Manage

Section 5: Working with the Media. Even as traditional media outlets decline, journalists continue to proliferate. Whatever their platform—Web sites, blogs, cable TV, satellite radio, or old-fashioned newspapers—plenty of reporters are eager to hear your advocacy message. Learn the opportunities—and the risks—of working with them.

Section 6: Word of Mouth. A skilled public official keeps her ear to the ground. If people are talking about your issue, you will get your target's attention before you even walk through her door. This section is a primer on generating "buzz."

PART I: THE MESSAGE YOU CONTROL

SECTION 1: MESSAGE FRAMING

To understand what framing is, it is helpful to begin with what it is not. Framing is not:

- Assigning blame or casting aspersions.

  Pointing fingers may make you feel righteous, but it won't attract support. Others will wonder if they are next on your enemies list.

- Demanding that you get exactly what you want because you are "a taxpayer."

  Virtually everyone, unless he is hiding from the IRS, is a taxpayer. The fact that someone complies with tax laws does not automatically confer legitimacy on his lobbying request.

- Complaining about mistreatment by a government official or agency.

  In itself, this will get you little more than an apology.

Framing is:

- Putting yourself in the decision-maker's shoes.
- Conveying that it will help him to help you.
- Anticipating opposition.

Putting Yourself in His Shoes

Regionally and at different levels of government, issues and priorities vary. But the vast majority of public officials share a broad, community-service perspective and strive toward five fundamental goals:

- Equity
- Avoiding harm
- Accuracy
- Honesty
- Consideration of reasonable alternatives

Putting yourself in the decision-maker's shoes means adopting his perspective and expressing your needs in terms of one or more of these goals.

Example A: You want the mayor to initiate a "Buy Local" campaign for the upcoming holiday shopping season. As the owner of a downtown clothing boutique, you are, of course, motivated by your desire to attract customers away from the department stores at the mall. You are also worried about meeting payroll: sales have been down ever since the town's last promotion effort, a one-day street fair.

But your company's health is not the mayor's priority. Put bluntly, how you meet payroll is your problem, not his. To be persuasive, your lobbying points must be consistent with his perspective and aligned with his goals. For example:

1. The campaign will level the playing field for all small retailers competing with regional superstores (equity).
2. It will keep businesses and jobs from moving out of town (avoiding harm).
3. It will dispel the myth that local stores have little to offer compared with the mall (accuracy).
4. It will be a fulfillment of the mayor's promise to help small businesses (honesty).
5. It will boost the local economy more than another one-shot promotion (consideration of reasonable alternatives).

Example B: You are urging your legislator to repeal a state employment tax. Again, remember that your bottom line (boosting profits) is different from his (serving the interests of the community). Stand in his shoes, and frame points like these:

1. The tax hits small businesses harder than big corporations (equity).
2. Repealing the tax will avert layoffs (avoiding harm).
3. The tax does not contribute as much to state coffers as people think (accuracy).
4. By supporting repeal, he will make good on his pledge to improve the business climate (honesty).
5. Maintaining the status quo will do nothing to encourage growth (consideration of reasonable alternatives).

Look in Chapter 5 for additional, more detailed examples.

Convince the Decision-Maker that it Will Help Him to Help You

Start by revisiting your target research. Review what you learned about his interests, priorities, and voting record. In particular, try to identify his "signature issues," those he works hardest on and takes the most pride in. Can you link his advocacy to yours?

Let's say you are lobbying for more police patrols in the downtown business district. If his issue is public safety, there is an obvious connection. But law enforcement can also be linked to community beautification: the police presence would prevent graffiti and vandalism. Has he fought to strengthen the local tax base? You could make a plausible case that reducing crime increases the value of real estate.

If there is no meaningful link, don't invent a contrived or convoluted one. Instead, think in terms of how the official could enhance his image by taking the action you want—reputation matters to everyone. Stress the large number of constituents he would benefit. Articulate why this would set him apart from other officials. Explain what you have done, or what you can do, to call attention to his efforts. If the opportunity presents itself, praise him publicly for his helpfulness.

Also, remember that actions speak louder than words. If you offered to contact other officials or constituents, do it immediately—and copy his office on the email. If you claimed you would pack a hearing room with speakers, follow through.

Anticipating Opposition

No advocate can foresee every potential opponent. But every advocate should anticipate some pushback: in government, a boon to one person is often a burden to another. For example, you might think that no one would oppose your effort to cut commercial license fees. But if that stream of money supports the local library, you can be sure that patrons will fight for it. Ready yourself—and more importantly, prepare the decision-maker—for this line of attack by identifying an alternative source of revenue.

As part of your lobbying effort, try to acknowledge and counter any reasonable (even unreasonable, but imaginable) opposing argument. Even if there is no early opposition, remember that it can materialize anytime and anywhere.

FROM THE TRENCHES

When Idaho's state health officials proposed tripling the yearly food service fee to fund effective inspections, business owners rebelled. Gearing up for a fight in the state capitol, they denounced the proposal in terms like "ridiculous" and "excessive."

Surprisingly, however, press reports did not show a united front. At least one food provider defended the plan, saying "It's something I think is vitally necessary, to have these health licenses." That one contrary voice may not have hurt the restaurateurs' lobbying effort—but it didn't help.[1]

Talk about your issue to many different people—not just your friends—and take no one's support for granted. It is far better to be overcautious than blindsided. Whatever the weapon, defenses erected in advance are much stronger than last-minute responses.

Another important consideration in framing: should you portray your issue positively (as a gain) or negatively (as a way to avert loss)? Conventional wisdom suggests that it is always best to be upbeat and positive. In fact, some marketing research has borne this out. For example, one classic study found that consumers were more likely to choose beef described as "75% lean" than as "25% fat."[2]

But overall, the evidence is mixed. Especially in the field of public health[3], some negatively framed messages (urging some action to avert disease) have been more motivating than positively framed alternatives (telling people how to stay healthy).[4]

Your decision should be based primarily on what you know about the decision-maker. Are you lobbying him to loosen restrictions on home-based businesses? If he is a risk-taker, you could emphasize the potential benefits of attracting lots of new entrepreneurs (positive frame). But many local officials are wary of land use reforms; in this case, you might talk about people who are moving because they can't pursue a profession in their neighborhoods (negative frame). Again, try to adopt his perspective and priorities, even if they don't precisely match yours.

FROM THE TRENCHES

It is not unusual for a retail giant like Wal-Mart to encounter stiff opposition when attempting to enter a new community. To protect neighborhood stores, some towns enact so-called "big box ordinances," specialized zoning restrictions that keep the chains out.

It is far less common for a local business group to fight a big box ordinance. But this is what happened in Long Beach, California in 2007. The successful charge was led by Lori Lofstrom, a lawyer and small business advocate who chose to frame the message negatively: " . . . We didn't want the city council taking preemptive steps to tell people where they should or shouldn't shop, or what kind of business should and shouldn't come into the city."

As reported by the California Chamber of Commerce, "Lofstrom and many other local business leaders . . . pointed to studies that show . . . the real negative impact of not allowing such stores to join the community is the loss of all the new jobs that would be created."

The Long Beach City Council took note and voted against a big-box ordinance.[5]

Setting up a "straw man" can be an effective framing device. This means drawing a sharp contrast between your position and some undesirable, albeit unlikely, alternative. If you want free downtown parking, for instance, it could be positively framed as a customer incentive. To reinforce this positive message, you could then compare it directly to a negative one: in this case, the straw man could be a prediction that Main Street will soon be marred by empty storefronts if the town continues to impose high meter fees. But this approach will fall flat if the contrast is hopelessly far-fetched. As an example, it would be silly to claim that downtown workers will quit over this issue. While many officials are inexpert about business problems, few are naive.

Sometimes, you might be locked into a positive or negative frame because other advocates got there first. For example, they may have already defined the issue as businesses leaving the city (negative), not as opportunities to grow the firms still there (positive). If it is difficult to reframe a problem, shift your focus to the solution. Preempt your opponents by convincing the mayor that your plan (cutting taxes for everyone) would avert job losses more effectively than theirs (investment credits for a few). When you make your case, don't hesitate to criticize their idea directly; but be sure to base your critique on facts, not on hyperbole or one-upmanship.

TRY IT

You can frame virtually any issue either positively or negatively. But it takes practice. To help you get started, here are sample positive and negative frames for three lobbying goals common among small businesses:

1. Block a state regulation
   Positive frame: Businesses will operate more efficiently without it.
   Negative frame: The regulation burdens business with time-consuming paperwork.

2. Fight a county sales tax
   Positive frame: County stores can offer more competitive prices without it.
   Negative frame: Shoppers will take their business out of the county or online.

3. Support a town "Buy Local" program
   Positive frame: Residents will take interest and pride in local merchants.
   Negative frame: Without help, many downtown retailers could close.

SECTION 2: MESSAGE COMPREHENSION

How a message is framed is not the only determinant of its persuasiveness. Another is how well it is comprehended, or understood, by the recipient. Government decision-makers are awash in reports, recommendations, and analysis. To make sense of the information avalanche, they try to categorize and evaluate it.

One way to understand something new is to fit it into an established mental framework. For instance, to categorize the first car as a mode of transportation, it was described as a "horseless carriage." To categorize computer-based communication as a letter delivery system, it became "electronic mail."

In the same way, you can help the decision-maker comprehend your issue by generalizing it to a familiar category. For example, if you are lobbying for the "Buy Local" campaign, don't present it as a departure from the town's earlier events. Instead, ask that he support it as an extension or new dimension of an ongoing promotional effort. Now he has a frame of reference to use in evaluating the merits of your request. He can compare it directly to other promotion alternatives; better yet, you can come prepared to make those comparisons for him.

Comprehension is also affected by language. No matter how well you know an issue, resist the temptation to use an insider's words or abbreviations. You can refer to the "Buy Local" campaign as IMC (Integrated Marketing Communications) instead of calling it a small business promotion—but why would that move an official who doesn't know what you're talking about?

For the same reason, don't indiscriminately pile on the background data. While it is a good idea to offer additional information, there is a difference between offering and dumping. No one likes to feel overwhelmed. You have a better chance of influencing an official with a few well-chosen examples than with a briefcase full of documents.

FROM A DIFFERENT ANGLE

Question:

At the end of your discussion with an official, you are left with the uncomfortable sense that he didn't grasp what you said. What can you do?

Answer:

It won't help to verbally repeat the same message he failed to comprehend the first time, or to embarrass him by asking what he didn't understand. Instead, follow up in writing as quickly as possible. Simplify and restate each important point, and confirm any agreed-upon next steps. (If you perceive either a language barrier or a hearing deficiency, don't hesitate to request a separate meeting with his staff. There's a good chance they have dealt with comprehension problems before.)

SECTION 3: THE MESSENGER

You should make the initial contact with a target yourself—usually by phone, email, or letter. But as your lobbying effort develops, you can include additional spokespersons to reinforce, bolster, or add interest to your message.

To be persuasive, any messenger must have credibility—which is itself a composite of other characteristics. A credible person usually offers some expertise, but she is also trustworthy and likable. A strength in one of these areas can compensate for a weakness in another. But think about it from a common-sense perspective: if you distrust and dislike someone, how much will you believe her?

Expertise can be established in different ways. Often, the basis is simply experience—as a successful businessperson in general, or in dealing with your advocacy issue in particular. Professional certifications and academic degrees can be important; sometimes, it helps to be vouched for by another expert known to the decision-maker.

Likability and trustworthiness, however, are subjective qualities. In other words, they are in the eye of the beholder and can't be measured. As a result, you must rely on your own judgment, supplemented by the opinions of others whom you respect. In general, keep in mind that reputation matters. A good name in the community is a powerful stamp of approval.

One group of people who are particularly prized as advocates are called "opinion leaders," those whose knowledge of or involvement with an issue is well known and widely respected. For the same reason that toothpaste marketers solicit testimonials from dentists, you may want to showcase a local business or civic star who supports your cause (and is comfortable being publicly associated with it). In lobbying, some of the most persuasive opinion leaders are prominent corporate executives, former government officials, widely-read journalists, and heads of major nonprofit institutions like colleges and hospitals.

On the other hand, don't make the mistake of recruiting a spokesperson solely because he has a high profile in local business, philanthropy, or politics. In itself, his name recognition will get the decision-maker's attention (and possibly a faster callback)—but no more than that. In fact, if he is uninformed or unenthusiastic, he can actually damage your lobbying effort.

Be especially cautious about using young people as advocates. Children are easy to like and can enhance your message with their artlessness and sincerity. As mentioned in Chapter 2, a child's testimony in a personal meeting (or at a public hearing) can be invaluable. But even if she is as cute as Shirley Temple, your little spokesperson must be able to offer some relevant experience, knowledge, or insight. Otherwise, her appearance may be memorable, but it will not be persuasive.

Whoever delivers your request, it should be clear-cut, reasonable and actionable—and you should never end a lobbying encounter without getting a specific response. As in business, talk is cheap; you need a commitment. Will the decision-maker sponsor your bill? How does he intend to vote on the ordinance? When can you expect him to announce his stand on your issue? It doesn't matter how friendly or positive he seems—if he waffles or wavers in answering such questions, you have more work to do.

Follow up, and offer additional information. Then do it again. Don't worry about being a pest. As long as you are polite, you can be persistent without coming across as obnoxious. While advocacy may be new to you, remember that it is routine to the decision-maker.

A DIFFERENT ANGLE

Question:

A prominent expert at the local college has offered to testify on your behalf at a public meeting. But there's a catch: he expects to be paid. Would this hurt his credibility?

Answer:

The scholar's expertise may be indisputable, but an opponent could question his trustworthiness. If his testimony is for sale to the highest bidder, it may not be worth the price.

SECTION 4: MESSAGE STRUCTURE AND TONE

What a message says can be undermined—or underscored—by how you say it. This is true across all communication tools. While content counts most, a few structural elements can make the difference between a message that engages a decision-maker and one that alienates him.

1. Start by establishing common ground.

Almost every business issue has some broad, generally accepted parameters. For example, the state of the national economy affects everyone. Perhaps it is widely known in your region that certain industries are healthy while others are not.

Even if you disagree with the decision-maker on many points, try to set a constructive tone by citing one or two that you agree on. It will be especially helpful if you can refer (in positive terms) to one of her past positions or accomplishments.

2. Build your case gradually and calmly.

You won't win a new customer by throwing your product in his face. Nor will you get far with an official by thrusting a demand or accusation at him. Your lobbying effort will be advanced by the clarity of your logic—not by the intensity of your emotion. You are entitled to state legitimate complaints, but you can do so with restraint and a modicum of courtesy.

3. Avoid gratuitous criticisms and angry generalizations.

At some point, your stance may become adversarial. But nothing is gained by starting out that way. Putting your target on the defensive will not convince her that you are right—it will simply make her wary of future attacks.

4. Don't proclaim your dislike for the government and anyone who works for it.

You might view government as the enemy, but the official doesn't share that perspective. Denouncing her employer won't change her mind.

Try to take a team approach. Fundamentally, whatever your differences, you and she are on the same side; you both serve the public.

FROM THE TRENCHES

Government health and safety inspectors tend to be unwelcome guests. But some entrepreneurs have decided it's better for business—or, at least, less disruptive for management—to cultivate a positive attitude.

[Local restaurateurs] Brenda and Bill Egenlauf don't see the Knox County Health Department's food service inspectors as an inconvenience. "One of the inspectors remarked that when she walks in, nobody runs to our kitchen and announces 'The health department is here.' We just make sure the issues on the inspection report are part of our culture."

[They] see the sanitarians . . . as a safeguard for their business.

"The health department is not our enemy," Egenlauf said. "We embrace what they do."[6]

5. State up front why you are writing (or visiting), and end with your desired next step.

Remember that a government official faces a daily barrage of communications. Make yours easy to understand. If you writing to request a meeting, say so. If you hope to focus his attention on a certain problem, or aspect of that problem, be explicit about it.

TRY IT

Regardless of which tool(s) you use to communicate your message, think about how its structure and tone could affect the recipient.

To get you started, here are two sample letters to a legislator. The framing and basic arguments are the same. But they come across very differently:

Letter #1:

As a small business owner in your district, I write to draw your attention to a procurement issue that affects many firms like mine.

I am sure you are aware of our local economic challenges, and the importance of small business to our state. As you know, the governor recently stated that two out of every five jobs in the region are in firms with fewer than ten employees. I appreciate the bills you have sponsored to help small business, such as your proposed entrepreneur "boot camps."

But we face a serious problem with state procurement. Specifically, it is hard for small businesses to compete for state contracts because potential vendors must document over $1 million in previous sales to the government. In effect, this requirement locks out many companies with strong track records in the private sector. These firms have not been public vendors in the past, but can offer new products and fresh thinking.

I look forward to meeting with you to discuss potential procurement reforms.

Letter #2:

I am tired of the "insider trading" in state procurement! I am a small business owner in your district who has sold my product successfully to private customers for 20 years. There are many firms in the same situation, and we want answers. Why are we prevented from competing for public contracts?

These are tough times for our regional economy. You people in government need to wake up! Even the governor says that small businesses like ours generate a lot of jobs in this state. You need our ideas and new products.

I demand to meet with you and I want to know what you will do for us beside sponsoring entrepreneur "boot camps."

Again, put yourself in the decision-maker's shoes. Which letter would be a better way to begin a relationship?

A DIFFERENT ANGLE

Question:
You have taken great pains to be pleasant and courteous in multiple lobbying encounters with a city alderman. That's why you are shocked when he starts to yell obscenities at you. How should you react?

Answer:
Stay on the high ground—don't yell back. Keep your composure and end the encounter immediately. Abusive behavior by a public official should never be tolerated or overlooked. Document what happened, share your experience with others, and—unless you get a sincere apology—find an alternate target.

The Five Biggest Message Mistakes

Mistake #1: Confusing a Slogan with a Message

Catchy slogans or acronyms will often win smiles. Just don't count on them to win votes. If you are creative, use your talent: creativity can make your message distinctive and memorable. But taken alone, it will not be convincing. In fact, a message that is overly precious can come across as insincere or hollow.

Mistake #2: Exaggerating or Distorting the Facts

When exposed—and it is always exposed—any type of misrepresentation will destroy your credibility. This goes for your spokespersons, too. In today's world, nothing is so obscure or hard to track down that you can get away with misstating, plagiarizing, or embellishing it.

Mistake #3: Being Inconsistent Across Time, Tools, or Messengers

Once you develop a well-framed, fact-based message, stick to it. Make sure the same arguments are repeated, and the same points emphasized, in every type of communication and by every messenger. Unless you have new information—or need to correct an error—there is no benefit to changing your message over time.

On the contrary, there is a downside. At best, inconsistencies will be distracting to your recipient; at worst, they may cause him to question the veracity of your message as a whole.

It can be challenging to enforce message discipline, especially when you have multiple spokespersons or a prolonged advocacy effort. One technique is to develop "talking points," a summary list of key arguments, to be used by all advocates (including you) in every lobbying encounter. As discussed in the next section, talking points are also useful for interviews with the press. Look in the Appendix for a model.

Mistake #4: Expecting a Target to "Take Your Word for It," Especially if You Are Challenging Conventional Wisdom

Education is a critical part of successful lobbying. No one in government is omniscient, and most officials welcome opportunities to learn about unfamiliar topics.

But unless you are a recognized expert on the subject—and sometimes, even if you are—your opinion alone will not change minds. It certainly will not convince someone to reject a long-held assumption. As solidly as possible, ground your key arguments in verifiable, independent research. If your target seems skeptical, don't get angry—get better information.

FROM THE TRENCHES

New York City Mayor Michael Bloomberg takes every opportunity to remind lobbyists of the importance of research. "We always have the saying, 'In God we trust, everybody else bring data,'" said Bloomberg.[7]

Mistake #5: Focusing Solely on Yourself

When the city health department fined your restaurant for a recycling violation, you fought the citation—and won. But knowing that it could happen again, you are lobbying to change the regulations.

In a case like this, it is important to broaden your message; it should be more than the story of what happened to you. Don't assume that one person's problem will justify a change affecting everyone. The mayor may believe that your citation was an isolated mistake—and he may be right.

Summary: Dos and Don'ts for the Message You Control

Do:

- Put yourself in the decision-maker's shoes.
- Show that it will help him to help you.
- Anticipate opposition.
- Review your target research before choosing a positive or negative frame.
- Be courteous.

Don't:

- Take anyone's support for granted.
- Use "insider" words, acronyms, abbreviations, or references.
- Use a spokesperson (no matter how appealing or well-known) who is uninformed or unprepared.
- Overlook the importance of consistency.
- Let anger undermine your message.

PART II: THE MESSAGE YOU MANAGE

SECTION 5: WORKING WITH THE MEDIA

No matter how persuasive, a lobbying message sometimes falls on deaf ears. It may be so controversial that your target shies away from it. He may get distracted by other priorities. Your opponents could have pre-empted you. Or, despite his sincere promise to help, a busy official might simply forget.

Transmitting your message through the media can elevate it to a level of urgency and interest you could never attain on your own, at least not in a reasonable time. Even with a high-profile tool like a petition, your lobbying effort will take weeks, maybe months, to reach a small fraction of the audience delivered by regional newspapers, TV, or radio shows. Public officials carefully follow these media as a window onto what matters to their constituents. In today's wired world, there is also a power-ful multiplier effect: news leaps at lightning speed from one outlet to the rest.

The drawback, of course, is that media messages can take on a life of their own. Once you have told your story to a reporter (or a blogger, or any other professional communicator), how he reports it is out of your control. The best you can do is to manage your media relationships. How-ever, this task is critical. The nature and quality of these relationships will determine whether or not you get the kind of serious, sustained coverage that helps shape events.

Creating Media Relationships

First, get to know the outlets in your area. Some are likely to feature more business news than others. If your issue has statewide impact, you will have a wide variety of print, broadcast, and online options; if it is local, you should focus on community newspapers, regional radio stations, and blogs.

After you identify some promising outlets, look for receptive reporters. Again, a statewide press corps will offer many potential contacts, and some might specialize in your issue or part of the state. Local journalists will be fewer in number, but also more accessible—and generally more knowledgeable about local people, places, and problems.

Read, watch, and listen not only for content, but also for style. For example, some writers always find a human interest angle. Others pack their stories with statistics. Still others like to use humor or provocative quotes. The better you can anticipate a reporter's preferences, the more effectively you can work with her.

To open a reporter's door, you can simply call or email her, introduce yourself, and volunteer to serve as a "source" for comment or background information. It can be hard to get the attention of a statewide journalist, but most local writers will welcome your offer: their stock in trade, after all, is a hometown twist on broader issues. You can also make your first contact by sending a press release, but be sure to identify yourself and provide your credentials in a cover letter.

As with other professionals, building a relationship with a reporter takes time. Don't expect her to trust you immediately. Many people like to see their names in print, and anyone can claim to be an expert on any issue. An experienced journalist will be skeptical and cautious, and it may take several tries before you succeed in getting information or a quote into one of her articles.

When you do get a reporter's call, follow through on your offer to be helpful. Get her what she needs when she needs it. Be scrupulously accurate. Keep a written record of your conversation and copies of any materials you give her, so that both of you can readily double-check what you said and provided. Remember that a professional journalist works under tight deadlines; she will appreciate promptness.

Especially if you are working with the media for the first time, you will probably hear that reporters are "biased." That is true: their "bias" is for solid, newsworthy information. Inexperienced advocates may complain that they are quoted inaccurately or out of context. Of course, mistakes happen; and some journalists are more context-sensitive than others. But it is up to you to be clear, precise, and truthful in every conversation. If you don't want something said or attributed to you, don't say it. If you're not ready to answer a question on the spot, don't answer it. Offer to get back to the reporter as quickly as possible with your response.

Media Time-Wasters and Turnoffs

Many novices waste valuable time when talking to the press. They may also undercut their own credibility and earn a place on the reporter's list—of sources to avoid. Don't spoil a potentially valuable relationship by:

- Engaging in small talk and aimless chatter.

  No matter how friendly she seems, a reporter does not call a source to make a friend. She is busy, and has a job to do. You can make her job easier by being focused and succinct, not by babbling about the weather.

- Telling the reporter how to write her story.

  Would you appreciate a customer telling you how to run your business? This is a sure way to alienate any media professional. If you want to help shape what she writes, give her the material she needs to write it.

- Dropping hints about some scandal or "big scoop," but providing no hard information.

  Few journalists have the time or patience for a wild goose chase. Tell her exactly what you know; she will decide how or whether to follow up on it.

- Failing to deliver something you promised.

  This is an egregious error. On the strength of your promise, the reporter might well have invested hours in research and other interviews. She might forgive you once, but never a second time.

- Complaining about other reporters or about the media in general.

  You will gain nothing from this reporter by trashing her colleagues or her profession. You may, however, make her wary of working with you. Why subject herself to the same back-stabbing behavior?

A DIFFERENT ANGLE

Question:

When you hesitated to discuss a contentious local issue with a reporter, he asked if you were willing to talk "off the record." What does that mean?

Answer:

In theory, it means that he agrees to use your comments without identifying you as the source. In practice, it may mean nothing. While some journalists are scrupulous about honoring these agreements, others are not. Even with the best intentions, he may forget, confuse, or misinterpret what you wished to keep "off the record." Unless you have good experience with this reporter or reason to trust him, don't.

Writing Press Releases

A press release is an opportunity to present your news exactly as you believe it should appear. Even if you succeed in becoming a trusted source for a prolific reporter, you will still need your own releases to call attention to what you think is important. While it can be as short as a paragraph or two, an effective release will whet the reader's appetite for more.

You need no special training to write a press release, but your topic must be newsworthy. This means you should be able to offer new information, a fresh perspective, or an interesting insight. If weekend shoppers in your town must pay to park downtown, for example, that may be a big issue for local businesses but it isn't news (unless the charges were just imposed). The news is that you have launched a petition drive calling on the mayor for free parking. Beginning with a headline like "Petition Drive Off to Strong Start," your release would provide the key facts—who, what, when, where, and how—and end by inviting the reader to contact you. You will find models in the Appendix.

Many local media, particularly online newspapers, neighborhood newsletters, or community blogs, will print your release just as you wrote it. So proofread carefully. Also, think twice about including your private phone number, home or email address. You can provide personal information to the media but request that it not be published.

TRY IT

Unfamiliar with all the newspapers in your state? Check the list on USNPL.com, the Newspaper List Page (and keep in mind that new online journalism ventures may pop up or disappear at any time).

Press releases are also accepted by statewide and national media outlets, but in a large newsroom there is no guarantee that anyone will read them. Targeting a particular reporter, editor, or columnist by name will maximize your chances of getting noticed; their specialties will be listed online, or are available by phone (in the case of television, look for producers on the news channel Web site). While it is time-consuming, the best way to spot a likely prospect is to read, watch, or listen to several days' worth of their work.

TRY IT

While major dailies are still hard to crack, the online editions of many mid-sized regional newspapers now offer sections of reader-generated content. Check Web sites for guidelines and tips.

A call from a journalist at a major media outlet is a big opportunity. But it carries some risk. While your topic caught her interest, there is no guarantee that her story will be similar to—or even based on—your release. Preparation is critical. In particular, if your news is controversial, you must anticipate opposition and be ready for likely attacks.

Here is an example of what can happen to your press release.

Your headline and text:
Petition Drive Off to Strong Start: Hundreds Want Free Parking
A petition to provide free weekend parking downtown received 300 signatures in 3 days, announced Jane Jones, the owner of Jane's Boutique and sponsor of the effort.

"This shows that people value a vibrant local economy," Jones said. "Hundreds are calling on the mayor to put out a welcome mat for weekend shoppers."

The petition is supported by every retailer on Main Street. It is available for signing at Jane's Boutique and at 10 neighboring stores. It can also be accessed online at www.JanesBoutique.com.

The reporter's headline and text:
Petition Sparks Questions of Residency: Mayor Asks What's Changed Since 2006
There are 300 signatures on a petition to get free weekend parking in the business district. But it is unclear how many of the signers—if any— live in town.

Mayor Smith is expressing concern about the petition, sponsored by local storeowner Jane Jones. "Of course I want to hear from our taxpayers. But there's no guarantee that this petition reflects their views," said Smith. "I know that many people who live on streets adjoining the business district are opposed to any change that would increase traffic in or near their neighborhoods."

Jones responded that she plans to alter the petition to require home addresses.

The mayor also pointed out that a ballot question asking voters to approve free weekend parking was defeated in 2006. Asked why she believes the outcome will be different this time, Jones had no comment.

You can be caught off guard no matter how thoroughly you prepare for an interview. Still, many major mistakes—like being ignorant of recent history—can be avoided by doing your homework.

A DIFFERENT ANGLE

Question:

If you have reason to believe that a reporter wants to ask you an embarrassing question, is it better to tell him "No comment," or to dodge his call?

Answer:

As long as you use it sparingly, "No comment" is a respectable, albeit unhelpful, response. Just keep in mind that the journalist may write "Smith refused to comment," which can sound like you were trying to hide even if you intended the opposite.

But dodging calls is worse, especially if you have any hope of building long-term media relationships. This practice sends a message that you can't be counted on as either a source or a subject. Also, you shouldn't underestimate a determined (and irritated) reporter: he could track you down in person and put you on the spot.

Staging News Events

A dynamic initiative like a petition drive offers the opportunity for a news event. This approach demonstrates your work in action. If your goal is to create a sense of excitement, a well-conceived news event will trump almost any press release.

Pick a time and a setting that will showcase your signature-gathering effort at its best: for example, lunch hour at your store on the busiest day of the week. Then invite the media. This time, instead of a release, you would send only a brief "advisory" including the basic facts and just enough information to be enticing. There is a model media advisory in the Appendix.

Think about the logistics, and plan ahead. Do you want clipboard carriers circulating through the store, or tables set up with piles of petitions? Should you have a sign at the door directing people to the tables? Are there enough pens? Minor details can be the key to a major success.

Because the idea is to demonstrate activity, make sure you have some. Don't leave the number of signers to chance; get commitments from as many people as possible to guarantee a well-attended event. It is also a good idea to provide the attendees with a fact sheet or talking points about the petition drive, as some will probably be asked to comment. Also prepare an information packet for every reporter (known as a press kit), including the petition, a fact sheet, and your business card. Get contact information from them, in return; you can follow up with related news, like announcing when you are ready to present the petition to the mayor.

You can build a news event around many different kinds of lobbying efforts. For example, a group of restaurateurs could stage an "Unhappy Hour" to protest a beverage tax. Downtown businesses could convene a "Save Our Sidewalks Day" to demand street repairs. Even a relatively small community meeting or rally can make a big impression on local officials if you invite the press. Be imaginative—and, as with all media outreach, be prepared.

Writing Letters to the Editor or Op-eds

These media devices give you more control than the others. Both are excellent ways to get your message to the public (and, by extension, to decision-makers). But beware: letters and op-eds can be condensed and heavily edited. Also, if controversial or confrontational, they are likely to provoke an opponent's response.

Letters to the editor are generally comments on a story, column, or previous letter that ran in the same publication. Some newspapers allow more text than others, but brief (about 100–200 words) is best; if you write more than 250 words, you are inviting an editor's cuts. Make no more than a couple of points per letter, and don't waste words on tangential metaphors, allusions, or jokes. Be aware that any individual writer may be restricted to one published letter per month.

Check Web sites for where to send a letter and how to find out when (or if) it will be published. Also, keep in mind that most newspapers have strict rules for verifying authorship. If you don't provide a phone number, they may automatically discard your submission.

TRY IT

A variation on writing a traditional letter is to post a comment on the online version of a story or column, or on a reporter's blog. You can try this in addition to, or as a warm-up for, your other submissions.

A downside to the online approach is that your contribution can get lost amidst a barrage of other postings. One way to call attention to your comment is to offer links to related material.

Another option on some newspaper Web sites is a small business "forum," a registrants-only chat room. The threads on forum topics can be educational. However, because contributions are anonymous, it is impossible to gauge their veracity.

A DIFFERENT ANGLE

Question:

Is it a good idea to get your friends, colleagues, and employees to send letters to the editor that echo yours?

Answer:

Yes, as long as they are willing to put some effort into their submissions. "Echo" doesn't mean "repeat" or even "paraphrase." To be effective, letter-writers must come up with their own ideas and words. No letters editor will be impressed by an armload of cookie-cutter missives; out of the whole batch, you'll be lucky if she publishes one or two.

An op-ed is an article that runs in the opinions and editorials section of the newspaper. Because it is longer than a letter, this format allows you to make a stronger, more detailed case. It is particularly effective when you need to refute multiple opponents.

To avoid getting your op-ed deeply cut—or rejected—aim for a maximum of about 750 words. Choose either a positive or negative frame, and be consistent. Avoid hyperbole, and double-check your facts. Be clear about who you are, what stake you have in the issue, and why readers should care about it. You will find model op-eds in the Appendix.

If your op-ed isn't published by your newspaper of choice, don't give up. Many editors receive far more submissions than they can use. Simply resend it to other publications. Small community publications are more open to new op-ed writers than major dailies, and also more likely to run your article in its entirety.

As with letters, newspaper Web sites will usually specify op-ed submission requirements and indicate how you will be notified of the publication decision.(If you're thinking of submitting to several papers at once, be careful: some will reject any manuscript that's under consideration elsewhere.) You can call or email about the status of your submission, but don't expect a busy editor to get back to you right away. In fact, many major newspapers state up front that you will only hear from them if they intend to use your material.

Whatever you send, keep a record of when, where, and to whom you sent it. Newsrooms can lose things. Also, you will need your original text to correct any editorial or printing errors.

Calling In To Talk Radio

With thousands of call-in shows around the country, talk radio has become a national megaphone. Its ubiquity, popularity and accessibility make it a uniquely tempting outlet. But as with other media, research and planning are the keys to using it well.

Start by familiarizing yourself with show topics, formats, and (where relevant) political slants. Even among business-focused programs, there are wide variations. Getting on the air is not enough; your goal is to get positive exposure for your message among an audience that matters to your lobbying target (even better, you can hope to be heard by the target himself).

The tricky part of a call is anticipating the demeanor of the host. Differences in on-air personalities are stark, more so than in program substance. Some will joke with you; others will challenge you on every point; still others make a career of being rude and sarcastic. There is only one constant: talk show hosts are entertainers. They like animated, outspoken guests. But you should hold off on making the call until you know what to expect—and you feel prepared, as much as possible, to handle it.

No matter how well versed you are in the subject, never call a talk show without a fact sheet or other documents in front of you. Once you're on the air, it is easy to get rattled, distracted, or just plain nervous; glancing at your materials will get you back on track. Also, keep in mind that your segment will probably last less than a minute. That includes bantering with the host—so try to limit the small talk.

Check station Web sites for call-in rules specific to each show. But in general, you should adhere to these guidelines:

- Unless you are under time pressure, avoid calling from your car. Not only is it potentially dangerous, but you may get a weak or unstable connection.
- If you don't get through the first time (or the second, or third), keep trying. Popular shows are deluged by calls.

- Hosts don't answer the phones. Your initial contact will be with a "screener," the gatekeeper for on-air guests. Answer his questions as enthusiastically as if you were already on the show; how you come across to him will determine whether or not you get there.
- Pick one or two of your key points to emphasize. More than that will be too much for such a brief interchange.
- From the moment you reach the host, stay focused on your message. Don't worry if he disagrees with you; that's his way of keeping the show interesting. Speak clearly, make your points, respond to any challenges, and say thank you.

TRY IT

To locate talk radio stations throughout your region, try the U.S. Associations of Broadcasters' state-by-state online directory. It describes the format of each station (talk, music, sports, etc.), gives contact information, and offers live audio links where available.

SECTION 6: WORD OF MOUTH

There is a cardinal rule for success as a public official: when people are talking, you need to know what they are talking about. This opens a roundabout lobbying route. If it is hard to get your target's attention, get the attention of others who will spread the word, both online and in person, through their own organizations, networks, and neighborhoods.

Civic leaders will generate the most buzz, but you should also encourage your customers, employees, and friends to talk up your effort. Get the message out to all your connections in sports, school, church, and social groups. Even if you've never discussed local issues on the Little League field or at the grocery store, don't be shy. You will be surprised at how many people take a strong interest—after all, their businesses and quality of life could eventually face the same problems as yours.

Like media, word-of-mouth communication cannot be controlled. But that weakness is offset by two important strengths: credibility and relevance. If a newspaper reports that you are lobbying the mayor for streetlights to reduce downtown crime, readers may or may not take notice. But when residents start telling each other to support your cause, their collective message will resonate—not only with other residents, but ultimately at City Hall.

A DIFFERENT ANGLE

Question:

An increasing number of print, broadcast, and online media have a clear ideological slant or strong positions on issues. If you know up front that the editors, producers, or hosts are hostile to your point of view, is it worth approaching the outlet anyway?

Answer:

Most of the time, yes. A news venue of any size reaches a large, diverse audience—some of whom will agree with you.

A possible exception: some talk radio hosts will not hesitate to insult and ridicule callers they disagree with. Their shows are still good opportunities to get heard by a wide audience, but you must be ready to deal with the abuse.

Summary: Dos and Don'ts for the Message You Manage

Do:

- Get to know the media outlets in your region; research the specialties and styles of their reporters and commentators.
- Explore op-ed and letter opportunities.
- Keep a record of anything you say and all materials you send to the media.
- Be creative about potential news events.
- Talk up your issue to everyone you know.

Don't:

- Expect journalists to trust you immediately.
- Stray from the truth (ever!).
- Submit a press release until you are prepared to respond to the opposition.
- Make promises you can't keep.

- Fume about "media bias"; if you don't like a story, give the reporter what she needs to write a better one.

Now that you have a working knowledge of the mechanics of lobbying, you can prepare to meet its broader challenges. The tripwires of politics, ethics, and other issues lie ahead. In the next chapter, you will learn how to safely circumvent them.

FOUR

Other Considerations

Any activity that influences public policy can cause ripple effects. Lobbying often gets entangled with politics. It can cause ethical quandaries. Your advocacy may attract unflattering media attention. But it will also give you knowledge and skills that can help you compete in the enormous—and sometimes baffling—government marketplace.

Section 1: Pros and Cons of Getting Involved in Politics. For some people, there is a natural progression from lobbying to politics; as you come to know a state lawmaker, for instance, you may feel strongly that she deserves (or does not deserve) reelection to the legislature. Other advocates give money or time to a political campaign simply to get access to the candidate. Whether or not you choose this route, this section will help you make an informed decision.

Section 2: Lobbying Ethics. In government, the perception of integrity is as important as the reality. For that reason, public officials—and those who lobby them—are held to higher ethics standards than most private decision-makers. The majority of lobbying regulations are designed for professionals, but you need to be familiar with common expectations and sensitive to potential conflicts.

Section 3: Unwelcome Attention. As a result of your lobbying effort, you may get publicity you don't seek and mail or other materials you don't want. Here is what you can do about it.

Section 4: Lobbying and Government Contracts. This section will explain how your lobbying experience can help you nail a government contract.

SECTION 1: PROS AND CONS OF GETTING INVOLVED IN POLITICS

At a recent community event, you met a man who is running for a seat on the county commission. He seemed very interested in your plan to improve the regional business climate. In fact, he called you a few days later for more details, and this time he asked you to get involved in his campaign. "I will bring a business focus to county government," he promised. "Right after the election, I intend to fast-track your proposal." Should you believe him?

Your safest course: believe in his good intentions, but don't count on the best results. If he loses the election, he will be powerless. Even if he wins, unforeseen issues may get in the way or take priority over yours.

The bigger question is whether or not it is wise to choose sides in a political battle. There is no simple answer: every race is different, and every candidate deserves to be considered on his merits. But don't allow yourself to be talked into any political activity that makes you uncomfortable. Before making a commitment, evaluate local circumstances—for example, whether other businesspeople are getting involved—and consider these general benefits and risks:

1. Benefits of Political Involvement
   - The candidate (and party activists) will be grateful for your support and inclined to prioritize your interests.
   - Assuming your candidate takes office, you will be "in the loop" of insiders who know first and most about what is happening in government.
   - You may make useful contacts among other politically involved business-people, civic activists, and opinion leaders.
   - You can raise your profile among potential customers and learn skills that can help your business.
   - You will get ready access to other candidates and sitting officials in your party.
   - By interacting with politicians, you will learn more about how they make choices and what influences their judgments.
   - By helping to elect a good candidate, you will improve the quality of government.

2. Risks of Political Involvement
   - You will make enemies in the opposing camp.
   - If your candidate loses, you will be viewed with suspicion by the victor.
   - To reap any benefits from getting involved, you will need to devote con-siderable time (or money) to the campaign.

- You will be solicited, repeatedly and aggressively, for donations.
- Your future lobbying efforts may be perceived as partisan, even when they are not.
- You could be assumed to support your candidate's overall policy platform or ideology, whether or not you do.
- You could unwittingly run afoul of one of the many obscure and confusing "pay to play" or other campaign finance rules.

What Is "Pay to Play"?

It is illegal for an elected official to trade public contracts or jobs in return for campaign contributions. But quid pro quos are difficult to prove. As a result, pay-to-play—a system of informal, wink-and-nod exchanges—is widely acknowledged to exist at every level of government. It is not only unethical and unfair; pay-to-play forces businesses to compete on a black market for contracts and influence. A report by the U.S. Committee on Economic Development crystallizes the issues:

> If public policy decisions are made—or appear to be made—on the basis of political contributions, not only will policy be suspect, but its uncertain and arbitrary character will make business planning less effective and the economy less productive. In addition, the pressures on businesses to contribute to campaigns because their competitors do so will increase. We wish to compete in the marketplace, not in the political arena.[1]

In their attempts to rein in pay-to-play, an increasing number of states, counties, and municipalities impose restrictions on political fundraising. While these laws help to deter corruption, their complexity also stymies donors who are honest but inexperienced. Moreover, the rules are wildly inconsistent—not only from state to state but sometimes on different levels of government in the same state.

For example, four states ban all corporate political contributions; five states impose no restrictions at all. In Pennsylvania, Ohio, Michigan, Texas, and eight other states, employees or officers of a corporation may donate to a registered political action committee, but not directly to candidates. The crazy quilt of penalties—for even minor, unintentional violations—includes a broad range of fines, sanctions, and imprisonment. Transgressors may lose government contracts and be banned from competing for future government work; in Oklahoma, making any political donation over $5,000 is considered a crime. The Appendix includes examples of some common pay-to-play restrictions.

Among local jurisdictions, too, there can be wide discrepancies. For instance, the towns of Aberdeen and Keyport are both located in Monmouth County, New Jersey, just a few miles apart. In Aberdeen, a government vendor may contribute to county political campaigns. But if he does, he could be barred for four years from getting any public contract in Keyport.

The bottom line: don't guess. Never donate to a political campaign, in any amount, until you have researched all applicable regulations. Remember that a sum considered modest in one race may exceed the legal limit in another. Under some circumstances, you might be courting trouble by donating at all. If in doubt, consult an attorney with expertise in election law.

TRY IT

Unfortunately, county and municipal campaign finance laws can be hard not only to decipher, but even to locate. Start with the Web site of your state's board of elections; type "campaign finance" into the general search engine. When you find the appropriate section, it may offer local links. If not, you will need to contact each jurisdiction separately. Actually, it is a good idea to do this anyway; laws can change quickly and unexpectedly, and at any given time, your state's information may be incomplete.

Also check the rules before you agree to make what is known as an "in-kind contribution." This is a donation to a political campaign of goods or services that your business normally sells. If you own a stationary shop, for instance, you might get a request to donate invitations for a fundraising dinner. If you are a caterer, the candidate could ask you to contribute the food for the meal. There is nothing inherently wrong with either of these donations.

But you need to keep in mind that the fair market value of an in-kind contribution normally counts against your overall contribution limit. In other words, if the pay-to-play law allows you to give only $300 to Candidate X, you can write him a $100 check and add $200 worth of free invitations— but you cannot give more in either money or product. (You can, however, volunteer your own time and unpaid service.)

It is not uncommon for a political candidate to ask his business supporters for free use of office space, telephones, or computers. Again, there is no problem as long as the value of your donation, in any form, does not exceed contribution limits.

If you belong to a coalition and are thinking of raising funds or endorsing candidates collectively—stop. Political committees (like their cousins, political action committees) must adhere to a special set of state (and sometimes federal) laws. In particular, there is a minefield of registration and reporting requirements. Do not take further action without legal advice.

Red Flags: Cash, Conduits, Campaign Loans, and Cyber-Deception

Steer clear of fundraising vehicles or promises that seem sloppy, unconventional, or unreliable. Chief among these are cash, conduits, and loans. Also ensure that your resources are not used for shady purposes like cyber-deception.

You should automatically turn down any request to make a political contribution in cash. The major reason is that cash donations are hard to track and verify. But cash is also tainted, fairly or not, by the fact that it is—literally—the currency of political corruption. For your own peace of mind and protection, stick to checks or credit cards.

FROM THE TRENCHES

There are countless examples of cash contributions gone sour, but some stand out for sheer brazenness—and for how much they damage public trust in the lobbying process and in the political system as a whole.

A 32-page indictment against former Massachusetts State Senator Diane Wilkerson reads, as described in the Boston Globe, "like a dime store political thriller." Among other offenses, Wilkerson was caught on surveillance cameras taking a $10,000 bribe stuck in a leather day planner, using a $1,000 kickback to go on a gambling spree, and stuffing $100 bills into her bra.

"Left behind ... were indelible images of Wilkerson allegedly accepting cash envelopes and vowing to work with 'laser-focused' energy to manipulate powerful figures and the state's political process."[2]

A "conduit contribution" is a way to get around pay-to-play limits. It can be a federal crime, punishable by up to five years in prison.

Let's say you support Candidate X but haven't made a donation. Another supporter—who has already given as much as he is allowed— offers to reimburse you for writing a check to the campaign on his behalf. "It's a win-win for both of us," he assures you. "I'll be able to do more for my friend, and you won't be out the money."

If you agree, you could be subject to federal investigation as a "conduit"— a person who deliberately hides the source of a political contribution. It wouldn't matter whether you knew of the scheme, or even if you were aware of the law. Take no chances: don't accept any reimbursement or other consideration in return for a political donation.

It is also bad business to loan money to a campaign, unless the candidate is a relative or close friend. While regulated, this practice is not illegal. The problem occurs after the election, when a loan can become difficult, sometimes impossible, to collect.

Although a political campaign can raise and spend more money in a few months than your business sees in a year, it is a short-lived, amorphous enterprise. Especially if the candidate lost—but even if she won—there will be few assets left after the votes have been cast. Despite her best intentions to repay you, political debts can be outstanding for many months or years.

Technology has enabled a new generation of political dirty tricksters. Never, ever allow your computers or other donated resources to be used for cyber-deception. Here are a few examples of these techniques:

1. Bulk emails: attacks on an opponent that are designed to look like they come from government offices, newspapers, nonpartisan institutions, or community groups.
2. "Phishing" emails: attempts to obtain personal information from voters without their knowledge or permission.
3. "Pharming": a means of hacking into domain servers to furtively redirect traffic among political Web sites.

Finally, keep in mind that political contribution records are public information. This means the amounts or kinds of most donations can be tracked by other candidates, political parties, the media, and interested citizens. Transparency is nothing to worry about, as long as the data are accurate. Just be aware that in politics, there are no secrets.

TRY IT

A key goal of campaign finance regulation is to help ensure a level playing field for those who seek public contracts. Current laws don't always work that way. That's why reform is a business issue as well as a good government concern.

Many business advocacy organizations have identified campaign finance reform as a priority for their members: two examples are the New Jersey Business and Industry Association and the Ohio Chamber of Commerce. If you are interested in adding your voice to this debate, begin by researching which business groups are already leading the charge in your state.

These warnings are not meant to deter you from supporting the candidate of your choice, but simply to urge prudence and due diligence. Also, remember that money is not the only way to help a campaign.

Ten Low- or No-Cost Ways to Contribute

First and foremost, make sure you are registered to vote! Then consider these opportunities:

1. Volunteer your time and talents.

Every campaign needs people with managerial skills and experience interacting with the public. Your contribution will be especially valuable if you can offer some specialized expertise or talent. For example, a volunteer accountant could keep the books; an advertising copywriter could offer to punch up the candidate's speeches.

2. Talk to your neighbors, colleagues, and friends.

In a local race, word of mouth can trump any form of paid political communication. People who know and trust you—and have done business with you—will pay attention to your opinion.

3. Host a meet-and-greet.

While candidates always hope to raise funds, they also recognize the value of small-scale, informal gatherings where the focus is on personal interaction more than money. Called "meet-and-greets," these are easy and inexpensive to organize in your home. You could also consider teaming up to host a joint event with a few of your business associates, neighbors, or friends.

4. Send emails to your personal contacts.

Because email addresses are generally not in the public domain, you can reach out to potential campaign supporters, donors, and voters who would otherwise be unknown to the campaign.

5. Put up a sign on your lawn or at your place of business.

Some municipalities ban campaign lawn signs, but most allow them on private property. It may seem surprising, but those mini-billboards can be highly effective in building a candidate's name recognition and in reminding people to vote.

Before you display a sign—or ask others to do so—check for any local regulations. This is especially important if you live in a condominium community.

6. Recruit other businesspeople to the cause.

In many local races, it can be enormously helpful to develop a list of businesspeople willing to make a public endorsement. Some of these individuals may volunteer to do more; but at a minimum, your list would enable the campaign to issue a press release announcing "Business Backers for Smith" or "Main Street Mobilizes for Jones."

7. Write letters to the editor (or call in to talk radio shows) to support your candidate and/or weigh in on the business issues in the race.

8. Speak to civic groups or appear at community events on behalf of the candidate.

9. Attend rallies, press conferences, and other campaign events where it is important to show strength in numbers.

10. Help get out the vote on election day; for example, you could call likely voters or drive people to the polls.

TRY IT

On the state level and increasingly in counties and towns, campaign organizations and political parties maintain Web sites year-round (not just during election season). Check these sites for information about candidates and issues, and also for suggestions about how to volunteer and what types of help are most welcome.

FROM THE TRENCHES

You can also choose to be political without being partisan. For example, a group of New York realtors decided to transform their offices into voter registration stations. The goal: to mobilize thousands of customers and other real estate professionals while getting the attention of candidates.

Prospective voters can walk into just about any real estate office in Nassau, Suffolk and Queens counties and fill out voter registration forms. Don't have a stamp? The Realtors will even mail completed forms to the Board of Elections.

... [The] voter registration drive also aims to enroll some 45,000 owners, brokers, agents and vendors, in an effort to "become a political force" against "regressive municipal land use policies."[3]

If you decide to get involved in a political effort, approach it not as a one-time fling but as an educational investment. Beyond its policy and partisan goals, a campaign is an exercise in marketing, management, and finance. In your own marketplace, its lessons can make you a stronger competitor.

Five Additional Precautions

1. Say you are a high-profile leader—such as a trustee or officer—of a hospital, college, foundation, or other nonprofit. It is prudent to check with colleagues to ensure that your political activity will not compromise the nonpartisan reputation or legal status of the organization.

2. If a friend or a member of your family works for the government, do not ask her to "help" your partisan effort during the workday. While most public employees are free to be politically active, there are strict prohibitions against using government resources, including phones

and email, and doing campaign work on government time. (Federal workers face extra restrictions imposed by the Hatch Act.)

3. Certain industries and professions are subject to special restrictions on political activity. Two examples are municipal finance professionals and gambling contractors. Make sure that no such rules apply to your business.

4. If you are engaged in litigation with a public entity, ask the advice of your attorney.

5. If you are averse to publicity, stay away from politics.

A DIFFERENT ANGLE

Question:

Some local governing bodies and other public entities, like boards of education, are elective but nonpartisan; in other words, candidates wage a campaign but do not represent a political party. If you are thinking about supporting a nonpartisan candidate, do the same precautions apply?

Answer:

Yes. Even without a party label, candidates can be associated with a policy platform or ideology that may or may not be in sync with yours. Also, depending on where you live, pay-to-play regulations can apply to any kind of race. For instance, if you are a vendor for the local school district, you must research possible restrictions on what you can donate to a candidate for the board of education.

Summary: Dos and Don'ts for Getting Involved in Politics

Do:

• Consider both local circumstances and general risks.

• Recognize that there are many different ways to contribute.

• Think of political involvement as an educational experience.

Don't:

• Do anything that makes you uncomfortable.

• Assume that you must give large amounts of money.

- Overlook or underestimate the seriousness of pay-to-play and other regulations.

SECTION 2: LOBBYING ETHICS

The Current Climate

In the heyday of corrupt political machines like New York's infamous Tammany Hall, bribery and extortion were business as usual. In fact, pay-offs were so common that few government officials even bothered to hide them. But the machines are long gone—and so is the public's tolerance for lawbreaking as a tool of influence-seeking.

Since 2006, the FBI has convicted more than 18,000 corrupt public officials.[4] From Alaska to Florida, thousands have gone to jail. Every level of government has been represented in the sordid parade—along with some of the nation's most successful professional lobbyists. In 2008, for example, high-profile corruption allegations ended the careers of U.S. Senator Ted Stevens, Illinois Governor Rod Blagojevich, U.S. Representative William Jefferson, and Washington influence broker Jack Abramoff.

FROM THE TRENCHES

Unfortunately, corruption among influence-seekers is not limited to Capitol Hill. There are also small businesspeople who attempt to buy favorable government decisions with cash or favors:

A Blairstown (New Jersey) man pleaded not guilty yesterday to attempting to bribe Hanover's mayor with a $20,000 payoff in return for help with zoning approval to build a Quick Chek.

[The man] saw the bribe as a last-ditch effort to save the project. . . . He stuffed $20,000 in a brown paper bag, drove to the Rockaway Townsquare mall's parking lot and handed the bag to [the mayor], authorities said.[5]

Their fate underscores the high level of scrutiny now directed to the ethics of public officials as well as those who lobby them. Particularly in the past decade, the combination of public anger and stepped-up prosecution has spawned a wave of new regulations. While these rules are primarily aimed at paid lobbyists, not citizen advocates, it is important to be aware of them. You will enhance your effectiveness and credibility by adhering to high standards—and by avoiding inadvertent but embarrassing (and potentially unlawful) mistakes.

Also, it is safe to assume that ethics laws will only get tighter and more widespread in the future, particularly in county and municipal government. Forward-thinking lobbyists make it a habit to seek guidance before they act.

FROM THE TRENCHES

Fairly or not, the media have fanned the flames of citizen outrage at ethics transgressions in government. As a result, prudent officials have become extremely sensitive to perceptions as well as to reality.

For example, as part of the city of Boston's ethics training curriculum, municipal employees are instructed to ask themselves three questions:

" 'How would this appear to a third party?'

'How would this appear to a third party who is on a grand jury?'

'How would this appear to a third party who is a radio talk show host?' "[6]

The Roots of Temptation

Like many honest businesspeople, you may wonder if the focus on public ethics is exaggerated—or futile. Some argue that crooks will always find a way around the law, while upstanding officials and lobbyists are unfairly burdened by increasingly restrictive rules and expectations.

Here is why ongoing vigilance matters—and why you have a stake in it.

Corruption is as old as the Republic, but contemporary government has created a raft of new temptations. These are deeply rooted in two structural features: the fragmentation of local administration and the cost of modern public services.

In most states, government power has been sliced up among a bewildering array of towns, counties, districts, boards, commissions, and other public or quasi-public bodies. As an eye-popping but not unique example, New Jersey has 566 municipalities, over 600 self-governing school districts, and hundreds of autonomous transportation, development, and infrastructure authorities. From port and bridge commissioners to sewer and utility chiefs, this means that across the country, hundreds of thousands of officials have access to billions in taxpayer funds. With so many individual actors—and, in many cases, minimal oversight—the odds are overwhelming that some will give in to greed and avarice. It only takes a few to create a culture of kickbacks, which can all too easily corrode honest government and hurt good-faith advocates.

A century ago, America was a largely rural, agrarian society with relatively scarce public resources. Infrastructure was primitive, and the services demanded of local government (such as it was) were simple and few. Even the most venal small town mayor, for example, had little to steal. If he stole it anyway, the impact on residents was limited in both scope and significance.

Today, the public demands an unprecedented level of quality and complexity in the services delivered by local government. As expenditures have ballooned, so have the enticements to thievery. A modern mayor's perfidy may involve millions of dollars. Moreover, one corrupt act—say, robbing the road maintenance budget—can devastate multiple construction, engineering, equipment, and professional firms dependent on municipal contracts. Layoffs and cutbacks by these companies, together with a loss of public jobs, ultimately translate into fewer customers and higher costs for other local businesses—like yours.

Three Ethics Hot Spots and What They Mean to You

Public corruption has many faces. The FBI offers this overview:

> Embezzlement. Voter fraud. Subsidy fraud. Illegal kickbacks. For example, a health inspector might threaten to report code violations unless a restaurant owner pays a bribe. Or a government official might award a contract in exchange for free work on his home or some other favor ... The Government Accountability Office estimates that [tens of billions of dollars] are lost to public corruption and government fraud every year.[7]

Obviously, ethics regulations cannot anticipate or eliminate all of these crimes. But that is not their intent. They are designed to "guide the incorruptible and help deter the corruptible," in the words of a leading New York government ethicist.[8] Simply by drawing attention to risky behaviors, the rules heighten awareness of right and wrong and help people make better choices.

Gifts

Why There Is Concern

Prohibitions on giving or receiving gifts in the course of public business are among the most ubiquitous ethics restrictions. The toughest rules apply to professional lobbyists, but some also affect unpaid citizen advocates.

Gifts are generally defined very broadly, as any "items of value," but there are wide discrepancies in the specification of "value." A $75 vase, for example, could be accepted by many state legislators but must be returned by a New York City councilman. While some laws exempt awards, tickets, or meals, the most sweeping policies forbid public officials from accepting a sandwich or even a cup of coffee. Look in the Appendix for some further examples.

The utility of gift bans is often challenged by both givers and receivers. Critics point out—correctly—that few officials can be bought with a lunch. They add that working meals, holiday presents, and tokens of appreciation are customary in the private sector.

That may be true, but a corruption-weary public wants evidence that government enforces the highest possible standards. Today, even a whiff of impropriety is too much. Whether or not an official gets a box of candy is beside the point; what matters is whether or not he is for sale. Gift bans, at a minimum, provide some assurance that he is not.

FROM THE TRENCHES

Proponents of gift bans can point to plenty of examples of "generosity" gone awry. But the excesses in Jefferson County, Alabama stand out. When Mayor Larry Langford was indicted on a raft of corruption charges, residents learned that influence-seekers had showered him with $230,000 in clothes, jewelry, and cash—then profited handsomely from the county's multimillion-dollar sewer project. As the Birmingham News editorialized:

> Everyday citizens live in the real world, where friends don't buy you Rolex watches and more than $60,000 worth of clothes. . . . And give you $69,000 in cash so you can go buy audio equipment and pay off your old shopping debts . . . When citizens see public officials benefiting from arrangements like this—and rewarding their benefactors with our tax dollars. . . . They see it as corrupt, whether the law says it is or not.[9]

What You Should Do

Do not assume that the gifting practices in your industry match those in government. Instead, expect the opposite.

Ask about any laws or guidelines in your town, county, or state. If you wish to give a gift, follow the rules—even if they reference only professional lobbyists at a different level of government. These policies set standards of conduct that can be reasonably relied on to make all parties comfortable. If you adhere to them, no one will have reason to impugn your integrity or that of any official who helps you. (A note of caution: be sure to respect the spirit as well as the letter of the law. If the mayor cannot accept a gift platter from your delicatessen, don't send it to his secretary.)

Conflicts of Interest

Why There Is Concern

Consider these scenarios:

- Mayor Brown's teenage son works at your ice cream shop. You've been cited by the town for a health code violation; now you hope the mayor will intervene.
- In your lighting business, you use an interior design consultant. This consultant is the wife of your state senator. You ask her to help you get a state lighting contract.
- The zoning board chairman regularly shops at your paint store. Because he often sends you other customers, he gets a discount. When you apply for a variance to expand your building, you count on his support.

Each of these cases illustrates a conflict of interest. Whenever an official has a personal stake in a public decision—in other words, divided loyalties—there is legitimate concern that he or she cannot act impartially or objectively. The details don't matter: for example, the age of Brown's son doesn't change the key fact that you employ a member of his family. The consultant holds no office, but her husband benefits from her income. While the zoning board chairman's paint discount is perfectly innocent, it could be portrayed as a bribe.

Most officials with a conflict of interest will remove themselves from any decision-making role. Mayor Brown will not call the health department, the senator will refuse to discuss a state contract, and the zoning board chairman will recuse himself from the vote. Otherwise, each of them risks an ethics violation. Even if the jurisdiction has no relevant law, they could be accused of favoritism, cronyism, or corruption; and if that were to happen, your name would be dragged through the mud along with theirs.

What You Should Do

Conflict of interest regulations are widespread, but often unclear. That vagueness opens the door to many legal challenges. However, no one really wins an ethics argument; in the court of public opinion, both sides end up tarnished.

Take no chances. If you expect to lobby Mayor Jones, do not offer a job, service, or favor to him or to any of his relatives. Wait until your business is concluded, or until he leaves office. (Keep in mind that in this context, giving his child a low-paid summer internship is just as problematic as hiring his brother to be your company's CEO.) Conversely, turn down any request from Jones to hire or give preferential treatment to a person of his choice—including him.

Be on the lookout for other common conflicts of interest, like these:

- An official or his family holds a substantial interest (over 10%) in a company seeking to do business with the town.
- An official or his relative is employed by a firm seeking a permit, license, or variance.
- An official decision is related to a personal legal matter. (For example, a councilperson who is being sued by a car dealer votes against buying police vehicles from that dealer.)

What if you have a preexisting business relationship with an official you want to lobby? Be up front about it. Document the connection, whether or not you are required to do so—and offer to approach someone else.

TRY IT

Many local governments have their own ethics boards or commissions. While these bodies have varying responsibilities and powers, most are willing to provide general guidance to citizens. They can also give you copies of town, county, and state ethics codes and regulations. An advantage of talking to an ethics board—instead of to Town Hall staff—is confidentiality. Like attorneys, the members of these bodies are prohibited, or at least strongly discouraged, from sharing any information you give them.

Use of Confidential Information

Why There Is Concern

Suppose that as part of an urban revitalization plan, several city agencies will soon be renting office space downtown. But the plan has not been made public. If a municipal official with knowledge of this information were to tip off his friend, a commercial real estate broker, he would be in violation of the public trust. Should the broker act on the tip, she would be equally unethical.

A government official routinely handles confidential documents, from medical reports to credit records. He makes daily decisions based on data unavailable to the public. Ethics laws preclude the use of this information in any way that would benefit him, his family, or others to whom he has personal or business connections. While rarely equated with crimes like bribery or extortion, trading in confidential information is no less corrupt.

FROM THE TRENCHES

In local government, inside information about property valuations and land use plans can be worth thousands of dollars. It can also send people to jail. In Parsippany, New Jersey, a planning board official was convicted of trading tips and favors in return for at least $36,000 in secret payments. According to the indictment, the information "allowed [a developer] to scoop up property in the township's Mazdabrook section for $10 million. Subsequently 360 homes and condominiums were built . . . "—thus enormously increasing the property's value.[10]

What You Should Do

Beware of any government employee who offers you information in a way that seems furtive or unduly circumspect. If you come into possession of questionable data, keep a record of how you obtained it—and get legal advice before acting on it.

Disclosure

Why There Is Concern

The size, scope, and complexity of government can bewilder even veteran lobbyists. Citizens often feel shut out by officials they don't know, processes they don't understand, and judgments they don't trust.

While it is not a panacea, information disclosure opens windows on government and helps to strengthen public confidence. When facts are readily accessible, there is less room for suspicion and doubt. The importance of transparency, especially in financial matters, was evident in the earliest days of the Republic. In 1802, Thomas Jefferson wrote:

> We might hope to see the finances of the Union as clear and intelligible as a merchant's books, so that every member of Congress and every man of any mind in the Union should be able to comprehend them, to investigate abuses, and consequently to control them.
>
> Letter from Thomas Jefferson to Albert Gallatin, 1802

The form of disclosure most common among public officials is called "transactional disclosure." Its purpose—in the Jeffersonian spirit—is to call attention to potential conflicts of interest so that citizens, the media, and other officials will be alert to them and able to judge for themselves whether an impropriety exists. Here are three examples:

1. A code enforcement officer declines to inspect a condominium, explaining that he is an investor in the building.
2. A county commissioner recuses himself from voting on a road contract, disclosing that the contractor is his cousin.
3. Mayor Brown refrains from comment on the report of your alleged health code violation, stating that his son is on your payroll.

Another type of disclosure recognizes that citizens and private businesses have a stake in ethical government. Vendor (or applicant) disclosure can be required of anyone who bids on a public contract or requests a permit, approval, variance, or license. While less widespread than transactional disclosure, it usually involves a written description of any dealings or shared financial interests between the applicant and local officials. Sometimes it will also require, or at least recommend, documentation of contributions to local political campaigns. (You will find a sample vendor disclosure form in the Appendix.)

What You Should Do

Be proactive about vendor or applicant disclosure; don't assume you'll hear from someone at Town Hall about any requirements that apply to you. If you can't get or don't know some of the requested information, say so (in writing). It is also a good idea to complete optional forms, unless you have been advised otherwise by an attorney or have another compelling reason to avoid them.

TRY IT

Some officials in decision- or policy-making roles must file an annual disclosure of their personal finances: income, investments, and assets. These are usually available online, either from the jurisdiction or from a central state repository. Check the reports to get a sense of what they include; the information may help in your general targeting research, or to answer specific questions about where or with whom a particular official puts his own money.

The Three Rs of Ethics: Rethink, Refrain, and Report

Now that you know to be on your guard about ethics, here are three simple rules to follow if you find yourself in a challenging situation.

1. Rethink the situation.

First, check your facts, and make sure you understand them correctly. Then ask yourself: Is my information complete? Are the sources reliable? (Double-checking the credibility of a source is especially important in a politically charged situation.) If possible, get advice from others who have confronted similar dilemmas or worked with the same people.

2. Refrain from hasty action.

Allow no one to pressure or cajole you into doing—or saying—anything before you have carefully considered the alternatives. In particular, remember that what you say on the record (for example, during your testimony at a public hearing) cannot be erased.

3. Report potential wrongdoing.

Should you witness unethical behavior in government, the best way to protect yourself is to document what you have seen. If your community has an ethics hotline or other reporting mechanism, use it. If the act rises to the level of a possible crime, contact your state's attorney general.

A DIFFERENT ANGLE

Question:

As a long-established commercial property owner, you have always worked to build friendly relationships with municipal building inspectors. When a new one turns up, you routinely treat him to lunch. Is this a good idea?

Answer:

No. While you intend it as a welcoming gesture, the meal could be interpreted—by the inspector or by a suspicious observer—as a bribe. It isn't worth the risk.

Summary: Dos and Don'ts of Lobbying Ethics

Do:

• Learn about ethics rules and expectations even if, technically, they apply only to paid lobbyists.

• Comply with both the spirit and the letter of ethics laws.

• Anticipate that the future will bring more—and tougher—ethics regulations.

Don't:

• Take chances.

• Ignore the unethical behavior of others.

• Assume that private sector practices and standards are good enough for government.

SECTION 3: UNWELCOME ATTENTION

Bad Press

All sustained lobbying efforts have the potential to attract publicity. The techniques you learned in the previous chapter will help you manage your media message—whether you initiated the attention or not.

But there is no insurance against bad press. Any advocate, no matter how savvy or skilled, can be blindsided by a story, editorial, online comment, or blog post that is negative, uninformed, misleading, or just plain nasty.

You can't anticipate or prevent it; but you can be prepared to deal with it. While there is no one-size-fits-all template for responding to a media slur or attack, you should be familiar with the two basic schools of thought: the Engagers and the Non-responders.

Engagers believe that it is best to come out swinging. As soon as the hit appears, they argue, a victim must attempt to refute or diffuse it. The fundamental concern of an Engager is that bad press often feeds on itself. Left unanswered—especially in today's hypercritical media environment—controversial stories and damaging opinions can rapidly spread through the blogosphere and generate additional negative coverage.

Engagers recommend these steps:

1. Immediately contact the writer. Use the phone if possible, as an angry, intemperate email could be replicated and set off more attacks.

2. Correct his error—then offer information he didn't have or a perspective he didn't think of.

3. Thank him (as sincerely as you can) for his interest.

Non-responders take a more cautious approach. They worry that you will validate the criticism by appearing to take it seriously. Because most writers—and readers—have short memories, Non-responders believe that bad press will simply dissipate if you ignore it. Their advice: do nothing. A Non-responder would follow up only in the case of a direct challenge—if, for example, a reporter asked you to comment on the attack for a second story.

Which strategy is best? That depends on the situation, and on your own level of comfort with the media. Here are three questions to ask yourself before deciding how to proceed:

1. How much will the slur affect your business?

Be realistic. Of course, it hurts to read disparaging words anywhere. But if they appear in a trashy local throwaway, it may not be worth your time to worry. Even if the outlet is credible—do your customers see or care about it? For example, a blog oriented to college students isn't likely to make a serious dent in your kitchen-remodeling business.

2. Is there a factual inaccuracy or mischaracterization?

Most professional journalists are willing (if not happy) to correct a factual error. Provide the writer, or her editor, with proof that you are right and she is wrong. Mischaracterizations can be trickier; if she writes about your "exorbitant" prices, she may not care that other brands are costlier. You can try to set her straight—just do it politely. Be mindful that if annoyed, she could get nastier in future stories.

3. Can you turn the bad press to your advantage?

Let's say you own a hair salon. If a local newspaper reported that the city health department cited your operation for five violations, you won't gain much by complaining that there were only four.

On the other hand, perhaps a blogger called your stylists "the slowest in town." While the remark wasn't meant as a compliment, why not treat it as one? You could post a comment, agreeing that your patrons are never rushed: "Instead, our stylists treat everyone to a careful, customized beauty experience." Your response might not change the blogger's mind, but it could get you new clients!

TRY IT

Keeping an eye on your press coverage is important. But no matter how diligently you try, on a busy day it is easy to forget or to miss a reference. Sign up for a free service like Google Alert (www.google.com/alerts) to receive automatic notification of media mentions.

Junk Communications

They are the scavengers of the advocacy world: compilers of mail and phone lists who will almost surely find a way to capture your personal information no matter how carefully you guard it. Do what you can to outwit them; be cautious and sparing about the addresses and phone numbers you provide to unfamiliar organizations or activists. But expect to receive postal mail, spam, and calls from a myriad of groups and political candidates you never heard of—and be prepared with a few simple devices that can help dam the flood.

Postal Mail

You can register with DMAchoice, an online version of the Direct Mail Association's venerable Mail Preference Service. It targets unwanted credit offers, catalogs, magazine promotions, and certain other mail solicitations, like donation requests. Your name will be deleted from many national lists for three years. However, while DMAchoice claims that it can reduce mail volume by up to 80 percent, it exempts political material and is generally ineffective with small, regional companies that do not belong to DMA.

An alternative approach: go directly to the source. Just write "Refused—Return to Sender" on the envelope and return it, unopened. If this doesn't work, a brief but pointed letter should be enough to convey the message that you won't support this cause, company, or political party unless the junk mail stops.

Spam

It is worth taking advantage of the Email Preference Service, another part of DMAchoice. The eMPS will get you off some commercial lists. However, much junk email originates overseas or with irresponsible spammers and is currently impossible to block.

You can, at least, avoid making it worse. Unless there is a clear opt-out mechanism—and an identified, reputable sender—never reply to an unsolicited email. This is what the spammer wants: confirmation that he has hit an active mailbox. Also, inform every official and organization you deal with online that they do not have permission to share your email address.

TRY IT

In some situations, it could be necessary for you to give out an email address to many people or groups you don't know well—say, because you are building a coalition or spearheading a petition. Instead of using your personal or business address, consider creating a new one solely for this purpose. Just don't forget to check it regularly!

Phone Calls

Register with the National Do Not Call Registry, a service of the Federal Trade Commission. It will stop most commercial phone solicitations to your personal number within 31 days (business-to-business calls are unaffected). Your registration is permanent unless you choose to make a change or your phone is disconnected. Some states have their own Do Not Call laws that add extra layers of protection; check the Web site of your state's consumer affairs agency.

Both federal and state Do Not Call registries exempt political organizations, charities, and market/public opinion researchers. However, if you ask, many of these groups will place you on an internal (though unpublicized) privacy protection list.

TRY IT

*67 is a free service available to many phone customers. By simply dialing it before the number you are calling, it blocks transmission of your own number. Instead, the display on the receiver's phone will read "Private Call" or "Blocked Number." This device is particularly useful when you are returning a call to an unfamiliar individual or organization.

A DIFFERENT ANGLE

Question:

A group that opposes your lobbying effort has begun handing leaflets to customers as they exit your store. The material is not complimentary. When you confront their leader, he claims the group has a "first amendment right" to distribute anything they want. Is he right?

Answer:

He is partially right. You cannot stop the group from speaking out (or leafleting) against your position. But you can, in most circumstances, prevent them from doing it on your doorstep. Even if they are standing on a public sidewalk or in some other community venue, like a park, they probably need a municipal permit.

Summary: Dos and Don'ts for Dealing with Unwelcome Attention

Do:

- Stay on top of what is being written about you and your business.
- Take advantage of free services to limit unsolicited mail and phone calls.
- Ask organizations exempt from Do Not Call laws to include you on their internal privacy protection lists.

Don't:

- Get rattled by bad press.
- Expect to be able to stop all junk communication—in any medium.
- Give out your contact information more often than necessary.

SECTION 4: LOBBYING AND GOVERNMENT CONTRACTS

Even in a weak economy, government at all levels spends billions on products and services ranging from the mundane (light bulbs) to the esoteric (museum lighting consultants). Especially when the purchaser is a state, county, or town, a sizable chunk of those expenditures routinely flows to local businesses.

But it doesn't happen by chance. Unlike ordinary customers, government procurement agents are constrained by complex regulations. They will not just drop into your store to buy things off a shelf. To influence them, you must research their needs, choose the right communication tools, and deploy the best message tactics. Does this sound familiar? Basically, it is an adaptation of what you have already learned: the Target-Tools-Tactics approach.

So, by reading this book, you have taken the first step toward getting a government contract. However, you still must navigate a complicated process rife with red tape. Specific purchasing procedures can vary greatly not only around the country, but at different levels of government within a single state.

In the Appendix, you'll find a list of resources that will help you master the details of public procurement. Don't expect a quick read; this effort will take time and patience. But because of what you've done and whom you've met while lobbying, you have a significant head start on any competitor starting from scratch. Make the most of it.

TRY IT

Depending on the nature of your product, you could have better opportunities in Washington than closer to home. But if you choose to pitch to the federal government, you'll need to know its unique rules and procedures. On the Business.gov Web site, click on "Acquisition Regulations and Standards," then go to the section for small businesses. Also, keep in mind that all current and prospective federal vendors must maintain a business profile on CCR, the Central Contractor Registration database.

Target

Who in government wants to buy what you sell?

The first places to look for leads are the purchasing or procurement links now available on most state, county, and municipal Web sites. Some are more sophisticated and user-friendly than others—for instance, you might or might not be able to complete all registrations and bid documents online—but all will provide at least bare-bones information about how and what they are currently buying. If there is an optional "vendor solicitation list," take advantage of it to receive immediate notification of certain kinds of opportunities. Even unlikely prospects are worth checking out. As an example, your county's historic preservation commission, while focused on old objects, may be a customer for state-of-the-art security devices.

At the local level, be sure to think beyond the confines of Town Hall. Many contracts are awarded independently by other public agencies and institutions, like boards of education, community colleges, housing authorities, correctional facilities, libraries, and public arts venues. The court system can also be a major buyer of goods and services from local firms.

Explore the centralized databases that can get your business name in front of procurement officials around the country. Start with the federal government's Dynamic Small Business Search registry (accessed through the Web site for Central Contractor Registration). Additionally, more specialized databases are administered by the U.S. Small Business Administration: for example, SUB-Net will provide information about your business to prime government contractors who are seeking subcontractors, while Tech Net offers resources to high technology firms. If yours is a woman-, minority- or veteran-owned business, visit the SBA's Web site to learn about targeted programs and potential set-aside opportunities (state or local laws requiring a certain percentage of public dollars to be allocated to these firms).

TRY IT

How small is "small"?
The SBA sets standards defining the maximum size a firm may be in order to access its programs, financial assistance, and set-aside opportunities. The standards are stated either in number of employees or average annual revenue. But they vary widely by industry, so you should check the SBA Web site (click on "Small Business Size Standards") to be sure your business qualifies.

Another potential source of leads is Business Matchmaking, a public-private initiative sponsored by SCORE (the nonprofit mentoring partner of the Small Business Administration) and several large corporations. BMM offers regional networking, selling, and educational events designed to maximize face-to-face interaction between government buyers and potential vendors.

Most importantly, now is the time to knock on the doors of some of the officials (and staff) you've come to know. Don't be shy: ask directly if their board, agency, or institution is in the market for products like yours. Make them aware that you are a motivated seller, so they will think of you when future opportunities come up. Even if your acquaintances can't help you, they may be pleased to steer you to others who can. Thanks to the general knowledge and experience you've acquired, it should not take you long to establish a rapport with new government contacts.

Once you have pinpointed some promising targets, use the skills you learned in Chapter 1 to research what they do and which products or services they have used in the past. In particular, check what they have spent on prior purchases to get an idea of whether your prices would be in their ballpark. (This is public information; if it is not Web-accessible, don't hesitate to file a Freedom of Information request).

TRY IT

Check whether your state offers a small business mentoring program along the lines of Georgia's model "Mentor Protégé Connection," which matches large corporations with high-potential small firms. A mentorship with a company that has worked as a prime government contractor would be an excellent opportunity to learn how to pursue subcontractor jobs.

Tools

When you lobby, you are free to select your own tools. But when you compete for a government contract, there won't be a choice. You must provide exactly what is asked for: most of the time, this will be either a bid or a proposal.

An IFB (Invitation for Bids) means that the purchaser knows exactly what is needed and will choose the vendor based primarily on price. IFBs include detailed specifications for the desired product or service, as well as rules for preparing and delivering the bid. On a designated date, all bids are opened in public by a government official. Usually, the lowest bidder gets the contract as long as her firm is deemed capable of fulfilling it.

Consider the case of a board of education ready to renovate school playgrounds. If the members have decided simply to buy new aluminum slides and swing sets, they will likely advertise an IFB for that equipment.

But the board might be interested in changing its approach to student recreation. If they are open to innovative playground designs, they would issue an RFP (Request for Proposal). This signals an interest in new ideas and a willingness to negotiate.

When evaluating a proposal as opposed to a bid, a government agency has more latitude to consider factors like experience, reputation, and resources. Creativity—and salesmanship—count. Does your company build themed play spaces with recycled and organic materials? If you can offer strong references and a fair price, the board may choose your proposal over cheaper ones. But be careful and thorough in preparing your materials: no matter how appealing your product, a messy or incomplete proposal can cast doubt on your ability to deliver.

FROM THE TRENCHES

While it is not yet widespread, a growing number of local governments are experimenting with a hybrid procurement procedure called "expression of interest." Potential vendors are encouraged to submit preliminary applications along with prequalification information. From that pool, officials choose only the strongest candidates to prepare complete proposals.

The advantage to an applicant is that she will not waste time developing a detailed pitch unless she has a serious chance of success. The procurer benefits by homing in at an early stage on the most promising suppliers. In particular, the EOI process can mean considerable savings for businesses that would otherwise spend heavily on highly technical, complex proposals.

For example, the Miami-Dade Aviation Department took note of the $500,000–$1 million cost likely to be shouldered by firms wishing to bid on the redevelopment of Miami International Airport. To ensure that such an investment would only be made by those with real potential to win the job, officials put into place a multi-step EOI procedure— "costing hopefuls only $50 to $100," according to officials. By soliciting full-blown proposals from only five vendors, " . . . The idea would be to have at least a 20% chance of getting the job."[11]

A DIFFERENT ANGLE

Question:

A buyer for a county agency calls you for a "quote" on an upcoming project. Is this the same as a bid?

Answer:

No. Quotes are usually sought in the earliest stages of the contracting process, to help the agency establish realistic price parameters. But unlike a bid, a quote is informal and not legally binding. That means the agency is under no obligation to award you the contract even if your quote is the lowest they get.

Under certain circumstances, government may award contracts with no competition. These are called "no-bid contracts." While there is some variation, most state and local laws restrict their use to a few situations:

- There is an emergency or other urgent reason to circumvent normal procurement procedures.
- Only one company can provide or operate the necessary product (for example, because of patent restrictions).
- Only one company is deemed able to perform some highly specialized type of work.

Many no-bid contracts are awarded to responsible, ethical firms for legitimate reasons. Unfortunately, when the rules are bent (or loosely interpreted), some are not. The absence of competition is tempting to shady operators and corrupt officials. It can cheat honest businesspeople who are deserving of opportunities, as well as taxpayers who must foot inflated bills. When no-bid contracts are linked to political contributions—the classic pay-to-play scenario—the result is a serious abuse of public trust.

Because your lobbying efforts have helped you network with public officials and become known in government circles, you are well positioned to hear of no-bid opportunities. If you are invited to apply for one, there is no reason to turn it down as long as these contracts remain legal. But you have every reason to support proposed laws and ballot initiatives that would further restrict or even eliminate their use. In the long term, uncompetitive contracts corrode the marketplace—and the government. A level playing field benefits everyone.

Tactics

Much of what you can communicate to procurement officials is limited by their forms and technical requirements. However, there are key junctures in the process when you have enough freedom to shape a compelling message. These include:

- When you create a profile of your business for a database or vendor registry.
- When you write a proposal.
- When you talk to prospects in person or on the phone.
- When you attend a vendor fair or other outreach event.

- When you are invited to make a presentation to officials.
- When you solicit a prime contractor for subcontracting opportunities.
- When you network with other government contacts.
- When you follow up on leads with an introductory letter and/or marketing material. (See the sample letter in the Appendix.)

While the substance of a selling message will differ from a lobbying pitch, you can use the same framing approach discussed in Chapter 3. Put yourself in the decision-maker's shoes, convey that it will help him to help you, and anticipate opposition.

Let's say you are a small caterer with an eye on the contract to run a café in the county library. Based on your research, you know that the library board is worried about losing patrons to bookstores. They seek low-cost but contemporary fare that will help improve their dowdy image. However, they are already deluged with proposals from restaurant chains with impressive national credentials.

If you adopt their perspective, it could lead you to develop a menu of locally grown, home-baked items unavailable at other venues. Your proposal could stress the benefits to the community—and to the library's image—of supporting small, innovative bakeries, orchards, and farms. It could also take on the competition, showing how the national chains are out of touch with local values and explaining why your business model is better suited to this project than theirs. (Of course, your price must still fall within a reasonable range.)

While you are confident of your ability to fulfill the library contract, do not expect the board to take your word for it. Provide examples of previous successful ventures. Furnish a list of references. If you have a record of commitment to community groups or nonprofit institutions, especially in a leadership role, say so. Perhaps you anticipate partnering with a well-regarded local supplier or training students for culinary jobs; these are the kinds of value-adding details that could put your proposal over the top.

A DIFFERENT ANGLE

Question:
   You have been approached by a consultant who claims he has years of experience preparing winning proposals for local government projects. Should you consider hiring him?

Answer:

If you are short on time (or self-confidence), it makes sense to look into his services further. But no consultant, regardless of his skills, can guarantee that you will win a particular contract. If he "promises" results, beware.

Summary: Dos and Don'ts for Seeking Government Contracts

Do:

- Cast a wide net when seeking leads and prospects.
- Use your research skills to learn what your targets have purchased and how much they have spent in the past.
- Put the word out among all your government contacts—whether or not they are directly involved with procurement—that you are eager for business.
- Shape your selling message to emphasize your local perspective, experience, credentials, and reputation.

Don't:

- Be sloppy or careless when filling out forms and following procedures.
- Assume you must always be the lowest bidder.
- Assume a big company automatically has an edge over yours.
- Lose patience; making a sale to the government takes time.

FIVE

Sample Challenges

This chapter applies the Target-Tools-Tactics approach to a range of common situations. In the real world, of course, every challenge is different. But as you'll see in these examples, the building blocks for a persuasive lobbying effort stay the same.

Section 1: How to Seek a Variance. Your business is booming, so you have decided to expand your space. But because your building sits on an undersized lot, you are denied a construction permit. Another common case: you want to convert a spare room into an office. But home-based businesses are not allowed in your residential neighborhood. To remedy these situations, you must usually obtain permission from a local land use board. In this section, you will learn how to lobby for that permission.

Section 2: How to Fight a Local Ordinance. The old adage isn't true: you *can* fight City Hall. This section will show you how.

Section 3: How to Change a State Law. Many state laws go beyond macro issues of policy to affect the nuts and bolts of running a business. Importantly, state rules can expand, restrict, or create new market opportunities. This section describes how to lobby for such an opportunity.

Section 4: More Sample Challenges. Also among the array of common challenges are tax appeals, nuisance complaints, and bid protests. Learn how to use the skills you've learned in each of these situations.

SECTION 1: HOW TO SEEK A VARIANCE

To accommodate a growing number of customers, you want to build a bigger parking lot. You have hired an engineer, a contractor, and a landscape architect. While their preliminary work is expensive—design concepts, drawings, reports—you pay the bills without complaint when they tell you the project is shovel-ready.

But it is not.

At Town Hall, the building official takes one look at the plans and sends you—literally—back to the drawing board. The parking lot proposal violates a regulation in your zone, or section, of the community. Specifically, it exceeds the allowable maximum "footprint," a measure of how much of a lot may be covered by a structure.

Now you have two choices. The project can be redesigned by your professionals—at a substantial extra cost. Or you can apply for an exemption from the regulations, called a "variance." This one-time waiver is granted by a citizen panel appointed by the local governing body and generally known as a zoning board of appeals, or a board of adjustment.

> ### TRY IT
>
> For future projects, keep in mind that such predicaments can be avoided. Research the rules before you sit down with a pricey consultant—most zoning codes can be easily accessed on your town's Web site. Then visit the zoning office, ideally with a surveyor's map of the property. Staff will call your attention to potential issues. Importantly, an experienced eye can often spot alternative shapes or angles that would eliminate any violation.

Target and Tools

In this situation, your lobbying target is a group of citizens who function like a jury: zoning board members collect evidence to weigh the interests of your business against those of the community. As with other targets, you should begin by researching their previous actions. Has this board made any recent decisions on variance requests similar to yours?

Ask the zoning staff to help you pinpoint relevant cases. Then obtain the written record of those cases; take careful note of the board's comments and questions. If you find a clear tendency to challenge the replacement of foliage with asphalt, for instance, you may want to rethink the design of your project. Also, attend a hearing, if possible, to get a sense of the members' individual priorities.

Some zoning boards are particularly sensitive to what's called "visual pollution"—variances that could compromise an area's overall attractiveness. Others tend to value the structural integrity of buildings over exterior elements. Knowing such preferences in advance will be a great help in framing the arguments for your testimony. Together with your basic application, this testimony will be at the core of the board's deliberations. (Occasionally, a variance application will be deemed purely administrative in nature and handled in-house by staff. In this case, you could be informed that a hearing is unnecessary. Still, it never hurts to be prepared.)

While testimony at a formal public hearing will be your key lobbying tool, some zoning board members are open to informal meetings with applicants (some are not—you must check). If this is an option for you, be sure to take advantage of it. Use the opportunity to get feedback, not only on the proposal itself but also on the arguments you plan to make. Caution: no board member (not even the chairperson) can guarantee either an approval or a denial of a variance at this preliminary meeting. Regardless of how well—or how poorly—it goes, you must still strive to prepare airtight testimony.

Message Tactics

In general, zoning boards will evaluate three major factors. Your message must be crafted with these in mind:

1. How your variance would affect nearby residents and other businesses.

Because they are charged to strike a fair balance between an applicant's needs and the community's values, zoning boards want to know that you are not indifferent to the neighborhood. A willingness to anticipate and mitigate potential problems will count heavily in your favor. Could your expanded parking lot obstruct someone's view? If so, assure the board that you already have a landscape plan to screen it.

2. Whether the existing code genuinely harms your business.

If you can convince the board that your undersized parking lot is creating unsafe conditions or causing potential customers to drive away, you will get much more sympathy than if you want extra spaces just to enhance the resale value of your property. As municipal stewards, members appreciate that vibrant local businesses benefit the entire community. But it is not their job to make your assets more profitable.

3. Whether you come across as reasonable.

Like most government decision-makers, zoning boards are risk-averse. Members may balk if your request is clearly a major deviation from the code, but be willing to take a chance if they perceive it as relatively minor. If your expectations are modest and you are flexible within some reasonable range, the board will be more inclined to work with you than if you seem rigid and demanding. For instance, they might refuse to grant your initial request for three new parking spaces, but offer a variance for two.

However, even the most cooperative zoning board cannot bend its procedural rules, which are stipulated by land use law and must be scrupulously followed. There are different application and notification requirements in every state; before you file any paperwork (or pay someone else to prepare it) be sure you understand exactly what you must submit. A single error—like substituting a rendering for a photograph—can derail the entire appeal process. Conversely, don't go overboard. If the board in your town will make a decision based on preliminary drawings, why waste time and money commissioning blueprints?

You should also show the board that you have done your homework and understand some common zoning roadblocks. By acknowledging these problems up front (to the extent they are relevant) you will seem more like a knowledgeable partner than a myopic adversary.

For instance, your application may be affected by:

- A public easement.

    An easement means that a public agency or utility has the right to use your property in some way. Usually it permits access to underground pipes and cables, telephone poles, or electric lines. It could also provide a road or pathway into any community facility, from a park to a power station.

    A zoning board will not eliminate or restrict an easement in order to grant a variance. You will get nowhere by challenging it. But they may be willing to entertain creative proposals explicitly designed to meet your needs while respecting those of the public.

- "Nuisance" ordinances.

    From restrictions on noise to limitations on the size of delivery trucks, these municipal regulations are generally imposed to protect public health, safety, and quality of life. It will help your application to explain precisely how you intend to obey these rules; conversely, it can hurt your case if you ignore or seem to dismiss them.

• Environmental ordinances.

Also known as "green" ordinances, these rules are intended to prevent soil erosion, avert water contamination, and otherwise protect the integrity of natural resources. They can range from prohibiting removal of trees to restricting disturbances of animal habitats. In some communities, environmental regulations even govern the species of plants allowed in landscape plans.

As with all other potential impediments to your variance, green ordinances must be taken seriously. You should explain to the zoning board how you have adapted (or are willing to change) your proposal to mitigate environmental impacts and respect the local terrain.

Like any other advocacy effort, your variance request may encounter opposition no matter how persuasive your arguments. The best way to respond depends on the opponent.

If any zoning board member raises major concerns during a public hearing, your safest course is to address those concerns, point by point, on the spot. While you can offer to provide extra material at a later date, there is no guarantee that it will become part of the record and be considered by all members before they vote.

Objections to your proposal from neighbors are a different matter. Sometimes you can head them off, or address small issues before they become big ones. Also, it's worth being open-minded—someone else's idea might significantly improve your project.

As soon as you have some preliminary sketches, make a personal visit to each of your neighbors, describe the plan, and solicit their reactions. Short-term, this can mean a considerable investment of your time, but the outreach can have a long-term payoff. For example, you might find less concern with what you plan to build than how you plan to build it. Think about your project from others' points of view: Will the mess annoy customers at the restaurant next door? Could construction vehicles block access to stores across the street? Neighbors may have excellent suggestions for ways you can control noise, reduce smells, and manage building debris. After a frank discussion, potentially serious problems may be largely eliminated—in fact, you may find ways to improve the business climate for everyone.

Coming across as neighborly is particularly important if you need a variance in order to run a business out of your home. Many communities severely restrict commercial activity in residential zones: the primary issues are traffic, noise, and garbage. Your best shot at a favorable decision is to convince the zoning board that no one will be disturbed by what you do; this means offering evidence that your work is clean and unobtrusive. A single hostile neighbor could upend your case—she might complain about the one day you hosted a big meeting—so try hard to be courteous and accommodating.

What if a neighbor flatly opposes your project? As long as he lives or owns property within a specified distance of yours, he has a right to file a formal objection with the zoning board. Still, your preliminary visit can help. Instead of being blindsided, you will know and be prepared to refute his arguments. When you have demonstrated goodwill from the beginning, it may also be easier to agree on a compromise.

Learn the Language

You can communicate more effectively with the zoning board if you master some of their terms and concepts. Here are 10 common examples:

1. Buffer
A form of setback, buffers are distances you must maintain between any building on your property and a specified environmental feature or protective structure. Among the most common are buffers for streams and stormwater detention basins.

2. Conditional use
A zoning board may allow a property to be used in a way that would normally be prohibited in its zone, if that use can be shown to serve a public interest or otherwise complement the neighborhood. For example, a sidewalk cafe might be permitted as a conditional use on property abutting the entrance to a park.

3. Floor area ratio
This is a limit on a building's total square footage relative to the size of its site. It is usually applied to multistory commercial structures.

4. Footprint
Typically expressed as a percentage, this is a measure of how much of your property may be covered by a structure. For example, a footprint restriction of 25 percent means that your building cannot exceed a quarter of your lot. The purpose is to discourage structures that overwhelm their sites.

5. Hardship

If your property has a steep slope, rocky outcropping or other physical condition that imposes practical constraints on what and how you can build, this "hardship" can provide grounds for a variance.

6. Historic district regulations

In effect, these are zoning codes within zoning codes: they impose special rules on all buildings, both commercial and residential, within a designated historic district. Designed to enforce architectural consistency—or at least compatibility—the regulations may apply to any structural feature, from walkway materials to roof pitch.

7. Lot line

This is the property line establishing the boundary between your parcel of land and a neighbor's.

8. Mitigation

This is an effort to alleviate or lessen the impact of some undesirable condition emanating from your structure or property, such as runoff or an unsightly view.

9. Setback

A setback is a required distance between a building's exterior walls and the line that separates your property from a neighbor's.

10. Yard

The open space on a lot which is unoccupied and unobstructed by a structure is called a yard. Zoning regulations may require both a minimum size and a specific configuration.

The Three Biggest Myths about Seeking a Variance

To Get a Variance, You Need Political Influence

While zoning board members are commonly appointed by politicians, that does not mean their decisions are political. In fact, as quasi-judicial bodies empowered to interpret land use law, the boards must be able to prove in court that their judgments are fair and based on the evidence.

It would be naive to suggest that members have no contact with political officials. Obviously, the mayor's support of an application (or her opposition) will get the board's attention. But it will not do more, except in the rarest of circumstances; say, when a single variance could plausibly harm or change the character of the city at large (or if one of the parties is corrupt).

Should you meet with the mayor (or other local politician)? By all means, if you want to. But she will give you the same advice you have already heard: Educate yourself, reach out to potential objectors, and present the strongest possible testimony.

You Must Hire an Attorney and Other Experts to Make Your Case

Some variances are far more complex than others. Your preliminary discussion with zoning staff—and your meetings with board members, if you have them—will give you a sense of whether you will need experts at your hearing. If the board's decision is likely to turn on tricky points of law, you are better off bringing an attorney. Are there highly technical design questions? If so, include your architect or engineer.

However, some applications are so clear-cut that a professional would be superfluous. For example, it shouldn't take a lawyer to request permission for a brick wall where only wooden fences are permitted. Again, ask the staff; and if possible, talk to previous applicants. (An exception: if a neighbor has threatened a lawsuit, you need legal advice.)

Zoning Boards Have a Bias against Business

Zoning boards are biased against variances that would be detrimental to the community—aesthetically, structurally, or environmentally—regardless of the type of applicant. Conversely, they tend to look favorably on applicants who show appreciation and respect for the zone surrounding them. It is silly to fixate on imaginary prejudices; just make your case clearly, honestly, and forcefully.

Finally, remember that whether or not your variance is granted, you—and other businesspeople—have a right to call for change in the zoning code itself. Fighting a land use ordinance, or any ordinance, is never easy. But with a smart, focused effort, these battles can succeed. Read the next section to learn how.

Summary: Dos and Don'ts When Seeking a Variance

Do:
- Meet early with zoning staff (and if appropriate, with board members).
- Meet with your neighbors as soon as you have a preliminary plan.

- Anticipate and try to head off likely objections.
- Show that you are reasonable, flexible, and concerned about the community.

Don't:
- Spend money until you have researched the code.
- Underestimate the seriousness of nuisance and environmental regulations.
- Assume you are entitled to any variance.
- Come across as arrogant or cavalier.

SECTION 2: HOW TO FIGHT A LOCAL ORDINANCE

Located in a popular arts district, your restaurant draws a steady tourist trade. Like neighboring business owners, you have had little reason to complain. Consequently, you have no idea how to fight the town's new tax on food and beverage establishments. While all restaurateurs are facing a big bite out of revenues, most believe that since the tax has been imposed, there is no hope of getting it rescinded.

They are wrong.

An ordinance is a local law; it applies only to a town, city, or county. That means it reflects specific, local issues, which are easier to isolate and address than statewide concerns.

On the other hand, ordinances are the backbone of proud, distinctive communities. Local issues can get personal. When you take sides, you often encounter unexpected opposition. But you are likely to find surprisingly strong support, too.

Your neighbors are correct to point out that it is much harder to change or repeal an ordinance after it has taken effect than when it has just been proposed. That's why businesspeople should take the time to read community newspapers and blogs, join local commerce groups, and otherwise keep an eye on Town Hall. Skillful lobbying can overcome a timing disadvantage, but you must move quickly.

TRY IT

Many businesses are heavily regulated by local ordinances, particularly in the areas of public safety and health. If yours falls into this category, ask the town administrator or clerk to include you on the list for automatic notification of upcoming changes. Also, become a familiar face to the members of the governing body; they may reach out to you when developing future proposals.

Target

The governing body as a whole is your target for this lobbying effort. However, you should pay particular attention to the mayor, who may have some extra authority; the sponsor of the tax ordinance, who is, presumably, the most committed to it; and any member who seems likely to support you because he has, in the past, consistently been helpful to local businesses or opposed to new taxes.

As always, begin by researching your targets' actions and opinions. Minutes or transcripts of public meetings when the tax was discussed, including records of relevant votes, should be readily accessible online (or from the town clerk). Also request copies of staff analyses or reports. Check the archives of regional newspapers and community blogs for coverage of speeches, interviews, and other on- or off-the-record comments about the tax.

Ask business advocacy groups, like the local chamber of commerce, about their experience with each of the officials. Get pointers from anyone you know in Town Hall. When dealing with local government, it is not unusual to hear through the grapevine about internal documents, like consultants' recommendations, that haven't been publicized; if you get wind of something potentially helpful, don't hesitate to file a request for it under the Freedom of Information Act.

As suggested in Chapter 1, you should visit at least one regular meeting, preferably more, to get a sense of the officials' different personalities and styles. Pay particular attention to their interactions with the public. One may be impatient and prone to cutting people off; another may enjoy bantering and joking with speakers. Still another (and this is not uncommon) will sit silently, inscrutable and imperturbable. Knowing what you are up against won't make your task easier—but forewarned is forearmed.

Another key goal of your research is to learn about the meetings themselves. Every local government adheres to a fixed set of procedures. These are highly specific: for example, there will be one rule for getting on the agenda, another for making a general comment. Keep in mind that a mayor often has the authority to waive these rules, either on advance request or on the spot. (This can work strongly in your favor if, for instance, he is interested enough in your testimony to extend the normal time limit.) Additionally, the body as a whole can choose to schedule a special session or invite experts to address a particular topic.

When attending a meeting, take the opportunity to introduce yourself to key staff, such as the municipal clerk, administrator, and attorney. Always leave business cards.

A DIFFERENT ANGLE

Question:

It's rumored around town that the municipal attorney is the real "power behind the throne." People claim that the mayor never makes a decision without his advice. Does this mean the lawyer should be one of your targets?

Answer:

First, a general comment: While it is wise to keep your ear to the ground, don't get into the habit of basing a lobbying plan on unverifiable rumors or allegations. This one might be well founded, but another could lead you seriously astray.

More specifically, it is rare for a municipal attorney to meet with constituents unless requested to do so by an elected official. For one thing, if the town pays him by the hour, your meeting would be an extra cost to taxpayers. Also, no matter how outsize his influence, he does not have a vote. Your advocacy time is better spent with those who do.

Tools

This effort requires a combination of written and alternative tools. You will need to lobby members of the governing body both one-on-one and collectively.

Begin with an email or letter to each official. Summarize your key arguments against the tax, then request a personal meeting. You can use the same text for all of them, or customize it for any member you perceive as especially likely to support you—perhaps one who both voted and spoke publicly against the original tax ordinance.

The letter can serve as an outline for the testimony you will present in public. Also, condense it into a fact sheet to bring to your personal meetings. Consider turning the same text into a letter to the editor of the local newspaper, and distributing it to other restaurateurs to encourage their own advocacy efforts. Some of them might volunteer to team up with you for the personal discussions, or to schedule their own.

This situation is well suited to a petition calling on the governing body to rescind or reduce the tax. If the arts district is fairly small, and especially if you are well known within it, you can aim for signatures representing 80–90 percent of local establishments. Even those not affected, like retail storeowners, will probably sign an anti-tax petition—they don't want to be the next group singled out for a tax hit.

Alternatively, you could distribute your petition at businesses throughout the municipality. This will raise general awareness of the issue while widening your base of support. Just leave yourself enough time to collect an impressive number of signatures before you address the governing body; the total will serve as concrete evidence that you are speaking for many of their constituents.

Message Tactics

During your research, you may have found that certain officials have general biases against food and beverage establishments. For example, one could believe that bars encourage lewd behavior; another might argue that restaurants violate labor laws. You may get opportunities to address such misconceptions. But don't be distracted. Your message must address one or more of the core dimensions of every public issue—in this case, you should focus on equity, harm avoidance, and alternatives. Here are the key considerations:

Whether the Tax Is Equitable

Every governing body seeks to be fair to all constituents. If you can show that the tax affects some establishments more or less than others, the officials will pay attention. Can you demonstrate a disproportionate impact on businesses outside the arts district? Will the tax cause local chain restaurants to lose customers to franchises in other towns? Regardless of its overall merit, the tax will be hard to justify in the face of some fundamental inequity.

Whether the Tax Could Cause Specific and Significant Harm

Some of the officials, especially the sponsor of the ordinance, may believe that local bars and restaurants are sufficiently profitable to absorb a new tax. They could be unaware of actual profit margins. Perhaps they don't know that while revenues are booming in the town's average food establishment, so are costs. If the tax will be passed along in the form of more expensive menus, you could argue that it is not just a business issue—it will soon become a consumer problem too.

Also, thanks to the arts district, eateries in your town probably attract a young, hip clientele. The governing body needs to appreciate that when prices go up, it is the younger, less affluent restaurant and bar patrons who will decide to stay home.

More generally, is the arts district the economic engine of the community? If so, undercutting its economic viability means hurting the whole town.

Be creative not just in designing your message but also in choosing your messengers. Perhaps you could recruit some local customers to complain about increased prices, or even a tourist to warn that he might take his business elsewhere. Don't overlook your employees, if they live in the community; it is helpful to remind the officials that food and beverage establishments provide many jobs.

Whether There Are Practical Alternatives

Presumably, the tax was originally proposed because the town needs money. Your best chance to defeat it is to identify alternatives: either a different source of revenue, or a plan to cut costs. All of your suggestions must be grounded in facts and thorough analysis. Be specific, concrete, and ready to respond to the concerns of other constituents. For example, before you recommend slashing the recreation budget by 10 percent, be prepared with examples of substitute programs that are low-cost but still appealing. (Also, avoid blindsiding others who are working with you; make sure they know of your ideas in advance.)

TRY IT

Use your first personal meeting as an opportunity to test-market your message. Make this appointment with the official you have identified as most likely to be supportive. If one of your arguments doesn't resonate, ask him to help you strengthen it. He will appreciate your trust and confidence; there is no better basis for starting a relationship.

Even the most compelling message can meet resistance from unexpected sources, or based on unanticipated arguments. Don't be surprised if you encounter one or more of these common obstacles:

1. Misinformation

Government officials are constantly bombarded with information, in written form, in conversation, and on the Internet. Much of it is reliable, but some of it is not. The unfortunate reality is that decisions are occasionally based on "facts" that are false, "reports" that are fabrications, or "predictions" that are fantasy.

So it shouldn't come as a shock if, for example, the mayor defends the tax by asserting that bars and restaurants are "mostly cash businesses." Based on misinformation, he believes you will compensate by simply shifting more of your revenues off the books. When an official makes an incorrect statement like this one, don't take it to mean he is stupid or ill-intentioned. Instead, view the misstatement as your opportunity to set the record straight.

2. Pressure from other sources

The idea for this tax may not have originated with any member of the governing body. It could have been suggested by a community organization, promoted by a state official, or recommended by a consultant. Perhaps a staff member crafted it as a trial balloon.

It is also possible that the tax was proposed by an anti-business advocacy group—or by a single citizen annoyed about litter from a neighborhood restaurant. You may never know. Whatever the history, keep in mind that there *is* a history. If an official's actions or comments seem inexplicable, don't get angry or frustrated: just restate and reemphasize your key arguments.

3. Poor judgment

Personality flaws and bad judgment plague every sphere of human activity. Government is no different. You may encounter powerful people who are arrogant, obtuse, narrow-minded, or just plain stubborn. If, after several good-faith approaches, you conclude that someone isn't listening or can't be moved, cut your losses. For every unresponsive or dim-witted official there are many caring, intelligent, open-minded ones.

TRY IT

Your town is not the first to impose a restaurant tax. Can you learn from the experiences of others? An online search of relevant postings from around the country may give you useful insight into why these measures are used—and how to fight them.

Learn the Language

Local government-speak is wordy and ponderous. To municipal officials, the jargon is second nature; to you, it can be confusing and ambiguous. Don't waste valuable time, or risk serious mistakes, because of miscommunication or miscomprehension. Learn some of these key terms and concepts in advance.

1. Agenda
Most scheduled meetings of a governing body will have an official list of topics to be dealt with at that meeting. Often, the agenda is included in the public notice of the meeting; if not, you can usually obtain it from the municipal clerk.

2. Consent agenda
You may find certain routine or noncontroversial topics designated as the "consent agenda." This means that the items can be approved in one motion, instead of being voted on individually.

3. Executive session
At various times during a public meeting, a governing body may withdraw into executive, or closed, session. The public is not allowed to witness the proceedings or to speak; attendance is restricted to officials, staff, and invited participants.

Some reason must be announced for the executive session, but the wording can be so vague or convoluted as to be meaningless. However, a closed session cannot be used as a delaying tactic or to evade a public vote; usually the purpose is to discuss personnel matters or pending litigation.

If you need to know the outcome of a closed session, ask the municipal attorney what information can be released, when, and by whom.

4. Municipal attorney

Every local governing body needs access to an attorney. Whether he serves part- or full-time, this official provides legal advice, represents the municipality in court, and is responsible for preparing and reviewing ordinances and contracts.

5. Municipal clerk

This official provides administrative support to the governing body. Her duties will generally include arranging, noticing, recording, and keeping a record of official meetings; maintaining public records; and supervising municipal elections.

6. Municipal code

A code is a compilation of ordinances, organized by subject matter. Many older municipal codes are not digitized and can only be accessed in book form at Town Hall or in the local library.

7. Public notice

Government entities are required to "notice," or inform, the public of their meetings, proposals, and potential decisions in advance. The idea is to provide citizens with sufficient time to comment or protest. Notice must always precede budget votes, hearings, certain judicial proceedings (like foreclosures) and bids on public contracts. In addition, a "notice of intent" may be required in advance of specific actions, like imposing a new tax or changing a land use regulation.

Find out where and when public notices are published. Use them to keep abreast of what's happening in Town Hall—and in particular, to check when you can address the governing body. Also, understand that these requirements slow things down. Even if the mayor wants to rescind your tax on the spot, he can't act without proper notice.

8. Public portion (of a meeting)

Members of the public must be allowed to address a governing body, but there are widely differing restrictions on when, for how long, and on what topics. For example, the public portion may occur at either the beginning or the end of a meeting; its duration may be limited or open-ended. Sometimes, comments are only allowed if they pertain to items on the official agenda. In many towns, anyone who shows up is entitled to speak, but others require advance registration.

Usually, the rules will be available on your town's Web site. If not, contact the municipal clerk.

9. Public record

This term refers to any record, in any physical (and, increasingly, online) form, that is retained by a government entity and open to inspection. Typical examples include deeds, business licenses, and bankruptcy filings.

10. Resolution

While an ordinance is a local law, a resolution is a statement by the governing body to support or oppose some position or action. Often, municipal resolutions are directed to state or national officials, asking for their help with matters outside local jurisdiction—say, a resolution calling on U.S. senators to expand nearby federal highways.

But a resolution can also be a meaningful way to make a commitment—in public and in writing. For example, you could ask for a resolution in favor of your petition, or expressing the officials' intent to establish a fact-finding commission.

The Three Biggest Myths About Fighting a Local Ordinance

The Fix Is In

Many people are cynical about government, and for good reason. Unfortunately, a few officials, at all levels and in every state, routinely turn out to be incompetent and self-serving. But the majority work hard in the interests of their community, despite long hours and harsh criticism. Don't sell them short.

Your lobbying efforts will not always succeed. On some issues, you'll find your targets immovable. But it isn't because their decisions are made in smoke-filled rooms at the behest of cronies or crooks. That's the myth. It's because their judgment was not in sync with yours on this given matter at this particular time.

That's the reality. As long as your advocacy is thoughtful, respectful, and sincere, you will always have another chance—and you will be taken seriously.

Influence Is for Sale

Political campaigns cost money. When they are running for election, politicians always appreciate—and frequently solicit—contributions. But once elected, any public official who tailors decisions to his contributor list is not only being unfair to his constituents—he is risking a sojourn in jail.

Myths notwithstanding, few town halls are rife with corruption. While money can (sometimes) buy attention and access, votes matter too. Even with a fat bank book, every politician is vulnerable if she does a poor job representing the people who elected her.

If You Fight a Powerful Local Official, He'll Take Revenge

Just as there are venal officials, there are also petty and vengeful ones. But you have surely encountered unpleasant vendors or customers; you do business with them nonetheless. Whatever the personalities in Town Hall, you must stay focused on your issue. There will be plenty of time to deal with any fallout—after you win.

Summary: Dos and Don'ts When Fighting a Local Ordinance

Do:

- Observe your targets in action at Town Hall.
- Learn the rules for public comment.
- Focus on equity, harm avoidance, and alternatives.

Don't:

- Limit your efforts to only one member of the governing body.
- Get distracted by misinformation or misconceptions; just reemphasize your arguments.
- Give up if your effort fails this time; there will always be another opportunity.

SECTION 3: HOW TO CHANGE A STATE LAW

Working with private schools across the state, your company has developed an innovative lighting fixture for classrooms. It is cheaper, quieter, and more energy efficient than current brands. With a solid record of customer satisfaction, you get ready to offer your product to the public school market. Then you hit a brick wall.

It turns out that in your state, the specifications for classroom fixtures are prescribed by law. To change the schools' options, you must change the law. While your trade association employs a professional lobbyist, he works only on issues that affect the majority of member firms. This issue does not—so you are on your own.

TRY IT

If you belong to any state business organization with lobbying staff, take advantage of that resource. Even when the professionals can't work directly on your behalf, they can share their experience with different legislators and offer general advice about navigating in the Statehouse.

Target

Always begin by targeting a state lawmaker who represents your district. You will have at least one representative in both the upper and lower houses of the legislature; the best approach is to lobby each of them, one at a time.

Information about your legislator's background and voting history should be easy to find on the legislature's Web site. There will also be a list of the bills he is sponsoring, a key window on his interests and priorities. If the full texts of his bills (or any others you want to see) are not online, they will be available from the legislative "bill room" or office of public information.

State lawmakers tend to attract considerable media attention (at least, in comparison to local officials), so an online search is likely to be fruitful. For additional insight, find out if your representative was endorsed by state business groups in his last election, and how those groups rated his performance in comparison to others.

It is always helpful to watch your target in action. Schedules for most legislative sessions and committees are published well in advance. If you live so far from the Statehouse that a visit is impractical, check whether the Web site streams and archives audio and/or video recordings of these meetings.

Tools

As with a local official, the best tool to open a legislator's door is an email or letter. Make sure to identify yourself as a constituent. If your business is located in his district, mention that too. Then explain the issue, succinctly but clearly, and request a personal meeting.

While all face-to-face lobbying meetings are important, this one will be pivotal. Bring as much data as you can find to bolster your case, preferably from expert and disinterested sources. Begin by checking recent state reports on any related topic. For example, the department of education may have analyzed energy usage in public schools. These analyses are often downloadable; if not, you can obtain a copy from the department or request it from your legislator's staff.

In addition, look for federal documents: has the U.S. Department of Energy looked into classroom lighting? Can you locate a university-funded study of the issue? A special warning: do not go into your meeting until you have researched previous legislative activity. You can be sure that the legislator's staff will have briefed him on this history; it would be embarrassing if he were to tell you, for instance, that an attempt to change this law failed just last month. Finally, bring a fact sheet, or a condensed version of your presentation, to leave with the legislator or his staff.

A positive response could take three different forms. First, the legislator might offer to prepare a bill; second, he could promise to "look into it further"; or third, he may ask you for more information. In the first two cases, you should follow up and ask his staff for updates, by either email or phone (or both). If he requests something from you, transmit it in whatever way is fastest—even if that means making another trip or two to his office.

Of course, the legislator may express no interest. Worse, he could tell you that he will actively oppose such a change in the law. If this happens, avoid—at all costs—getting angry. You need to preserve his goodwill for future encounters. Make every effort to address his concerns, and end the meeting by thanking him for his time.

Then start over. Try to identify another legislator with a special expertise in education, or energy, who could be more receptive to your efforts. Repeat your target research, refine your tools, and remind yourself that lobbying success rarely happens overnight.

Message Tactics

Remember: you are lobbying to change a law that will affect the entire state, not just your company. This will be the legislator's perspective, and you must craft your message accordingly.

TRY IT

One way to get accustomed to thinking statewide is to read other testimony delivered during public hearings at the Statehouse. Check the Web sites of trade associations or business advocacy groups, like your state's Chamber of Commerce. Some post the text of recent testimony; others (even better) offer Web casts or audio transcripts.

As with most local issues, three core dimensions are equity, harm avoidance, and alternatives. But a member of the legislature—who can act only with the concurrence of other members—must ask himself an additional question: if I sponsor this change in the law, how many of my colleagues are likely to vote for it? He is most likely to consider:

1. Whether changing the law would be equitable.

The key here is to show that the change would not benefit your company exclusively, or give you an unfair advantage in the marketplace. Be careful to put your request in terms of increased options for schools, not moneymaking opportunities for your business. Ask only for flexibility in what the law requires; it must be clear that any of your competitors would still be able to compete for classroom lighting contracts.

2. Whether the current law causes specific and significant harm.

Again, keep in mind that legislators act in the interests of the state. You must define harm in terms of public schools, not in terms of your potential profit.

In this context, there are at least three possible types of harm. Your message should home in on whichever one is most relevant and significant in magnitude (though you could certainly mention the others). These three types include:

- Cost: Are schools spending more than necessary because they are locked into certain products?
- Energy: Do current school fixtures waste energy?
- Noise: Are current fixtures so noisy as to bother students or staff?

Of course, you are free to describe any potential problems your research turns up. Just be careful not to exaggerate or embellish your descriptions.

3. Whether there are practical alternatives.

The legislator's simplest alternative is to do nothing. That's why the burden is on you to demonstrate some shortcoming in the status quo, or an opportunity to do better.

You may be able to identify other practical approaches by researching how this issue is handled elsewhere. Can you find examples of states with highly flexible specifications? Are others in the process of changing their laws? Is there a model statute?

TRY IT

You can obtain information about other states by searching their Web sites individually, but this can be tedious. Another excellent resource is the National Conference of State Legislatures. While targeted primarily to legislators and staff, its site includes citizen-friendly summaries of state activity in every major policy area.

Finally, before making a commitment, your legislator will consider how much support he is likely to get from other legislators. You should assure him of your willingness to help. Offer (enthusiastically) to meet with others, make presentations, write letters, testify at committee hearings—whatever it takes.

No less than local officials, state lawmakers are subject to misinformation, pressure from other sources, and poor judgment. You can't head off all these problems—especially when they are statewide in scope—but you can prepare to refute your likeliest opponents.

For example, current lighting suppliers will probably argue against any change, claiming that their products cannot be surpassed. School administrators may be skeptical about potential savings. Even parents' groups could get involved; they might worry about the quality of the light. No matter what comes up, stay focused, be courteous, and learn from the debate.

Learn the Language

Certain legislative terminology is fairly standard across states. At a minimum, you should be familiar with these basics. There is also state-specific phraseology—and, of course, slang—that you will pick up quickly by spending time with your legislator and around the Statehouse.

1. Appropriations

The state cannot spend money until specific appropriations, or maximum dollar amounts, are authorized for specific purposes by an act of the legislature.

2. Bill

A bill is a proposed law. In order to advance, it must be formally introduced during a legislative session; at that time it is assigned a number and sent to a committee.

3. Committee

After it is introduced, a bill is sent, or "referred," to a legislative committee. Committees deal with specific policy areas, such as education, human services, judiciary, or health care. Because they specialize, committee staff are highly proficient in their areas of expertise; they draft bill language and serve the legislators as key resources and advisors.

Most of the analysis and scrutiny of a bill takes place during committee meetings. After the sponsor's comments to the committee, testimony may be offered both in favor of and against his bill. Then the committee votes; if passed, the bill can be presented for consideration by the full legislature. If defeated, the sponsor may choose to amend and reintroduce it.

4. Fiscal notes

At the time a bill is introduced, an estimate is made of its likely impact on state revenues and expenditures. Fiscal notes can play an important part in building—or weakening—support for proposed legislation.

5. Legislative aides

These are professional, usually partisan staff assistants to individual legislators. They are generally responsible for constituent services, media relations, and liaison with other legislators.

6. Legislative caucus

This is a group of legislators who choose to work together to develop, support, or defeat bills. Typically, each legislative chamber has a Democratic and Republican caucus, but there are often additional caucuses defined by policy goals, ethnic concerns, or regional interests. For example, your state could have a Black Caucus, an Environmental Caucus, and/or an Urban Affairs Caucus.

7. Public hearing

This is the opportunity offered to citizens who wish to express an opinion, pro or con, about a specific bill or issue under consideration by a legislative committee.

8. Session

A session is the period during which the legislature regularly meets and takes formal action. The dates and durations of legislative sessions vary widely around the country. Under some circumstances, a legislature may add additional, or "special," sessions to its normal calendar.

9. Sponsor

A legislator who develops, introduces and advocates for a bill is called its sponsor. Most bills also have cosponsors.

10. Statute

When a bill has been enacted into law, it becomes a state statute.

The Three Biggest Myths About Working to Change a State Law

The Only Way to Influence a Legislator Is Through a Professional Lobbyist

Unfortunately, this is a highly pervasive myth. Because of it, many businesspeople have been too discouraged even to try lobbying on their own. But by reading this book, you have learned the reality: a legislator, or other government decision-maker, can be influenced by anyone who masters the Target-Tools-Tactics advocacy approach.

Like other professionals, an experienced lobbyist benefits from established relationships and institutional knowledge. These are valuable, but not indispensable. Your expertise, passion, and hard work—the same things that make you successful in business—can also make you a highly persuasive advocate.

Legislators Are Not Enough—You Must Get to the Governor

Of course, governors wield great power. They can, and do, veto many bills that emerge from state legislatures. But for many of their initiatives, governors need legislative support. Politics aside, it is in their interests to work in partnership with lawmakers, not around or against them.

Unless your issue is unusually polarizing or contentious, there is no reason to assume the governor's opinion will differ from the consensus of the legislature. You could choose to lobby her directly, but from a practical perspective, legislators are far more accessible than governors. So keep the focus on your target. One success will lead to others.

All Legislators Are the Same—It Doesn't Matter Which One You Lobby

This myth is most often invoked in two cases: either your own district representative has turned you down, or you have some personal connection to another legislator.

If your lobbying effort has failed to persuade your own representative, you are, of course, free to target another lawmaker. In theory, this could work to your advantage; you might succeed with a key member of the committee that would hear your bill, or with a powerful legislative leader. But in practice, questions will be raised about why your legislator objects. As a matter of courtesy, he will certainly be asked. So you should make your first and best efforts close to home; at a minimum, try to reduce any major local objections to minor ones.

Personal connections are always helpful, especially for expediting and breaking the ice in an initial meeting. But the same caution applies: any other legislator will want to know the reaction of your hometown representative. As well as you can, be prepared.

Summary: Dos and Don'ts When Working to Change a State Law

Do:

- Target the legislator(s) in your own district.
- Think statewide.
- Prepare to refute your likeliest opponents.

Don't:

- Forget to familiarize yourself with any previous legislative activity in your state.
- Ignore the experience of other states.
- Exaggerate or embellish.

SECTION 4: MORE SAMPLE CHALLENGES

You have owned and managed a rental property in a resort town for many years. Until recently, business was good and expenses held steady. But an ailing tourist economy has cut into your income. At the same time, it has seriously reduced the resale value of your building.

Then your property tax bill arrives: you are dismayed to see that, despite the local slump, you are expected to pay more than ever. How can you challenge this tax hit?

There is another problem, too. Your tenants are complaining about the noise generated by construction on a nearby road. The ear-splitting din has gone on for months. How can you stop it?

Meanwhile, your spouse is exploring opportunities to supplement your rental income. Based on her experience helping tourists plan and enjoy vacations in the area, she responded to the town's request for a proposal to run a visitor center. Now she's learned that the contract was awarded to a competitor—who just moved into the state. This award seems unfair. How can she contest it?

Property tax appeals, nuisance complaints, and contract award protests are a few of the many additional challenges that could face your business in the future. While there are rules and processes specific to each one, it is helpful, again, to understand how you can apply variations of the same basic lobbying principles to this diverse array of problems.

Target

Basic Principles

In all three of these situations, there is a serious risk of misidentifying the target, thus wasting time and potentially missing critical deadlines. That's because of another similarity: the correct target is far from obvious, so good research counts.

The first step is to figure out which public entity deals with the matter at hand. Depending on where you live, property taxes may originate in different places and be calculated in a variety of ways. Nuisances like construction noise are usually resolved at the municipal level, but could involve a private party or another level of government. Some contract protests are handled by the contracting body, while others must be filed with a hearing officer or mediator.

Use the same basic resources and research model you've used before. Start with what you think is the most appropriate jurisdictional Web site; try to determine who is in charge of what. Identify the responsibilities of each division or office and scan Frequently Asked Questions. If your target is still unclear, contact someone who oversees matters related to yours. For example, your county's budget director could give you the name of your town's tax assessor.

The biggest mistake to avoid: don't fire off a bunch of angry emails to every important-sounding person on the Web site. Most won't respond, and those who do will probably just direct you elsewhere. This is a sure path to frustration and delay, not results.

Next, take advantage of other online resources you have learned to access: for instance, tax, zoning, or vendor records could lead you to the right board or decision-maker. Look in media archives for reports of problems similar to yours. Check the minutes of relevant public meetings. If necessary, file freedom of information requests.

Finally, go offline. Talk to knowledgeable people. Attend a meeting of the appropriate public body, like a board of assessment appeals, to observe its procedures and put faces and personalities to names and titles.

Specific Rules and Processes

Tax Appeals

The target of a tax appeal must be the official or board responsible for your assessment. An assessment is an opinion of your property's value that is backed up by evidence and/or professional judgment. Across states and local governments, dozens of disparate formulas are used not only to arrive at an assessment, but also to determine how and when it is reflected in a particular tax. Reassessments may be conducted annually or at much longer intervals.

But there is one consistent rule: while the action is known as a tax appeal, a property owner may technically challenge only his assessment, not his actual tax. This is an important, albeit confusing, distinction. A tax is the collective stream of revenue raised by a town, county, school, or other public body to fund its operations. An assessment is a measure of one owner's (purportedly) fair share of that tax. If you complain to the taxing authority, like the town council, they will simply refer you to the assessing authority, like the municipal assessor or appeals board. You will save time and aggravation by targeting correctly.

TRY IT

If you have trouble identifying tax officials, the Web site of the Federation of Tax Administrators is worth a look. Because tax laws differ radically across the country, the FTA may not have exactly the information you need, but it offers useful links to state tax agencies, publications, forms, and other resources.

Nuisance Complaints

Nuisance ordinances restrict not only noise, but also a wide range of other behaviors (like lewdness) or property conditions (like overgrown vegetation) considered to be disruptive, unhealthy, unsightly, or otherwise detrimental to the community. While these laws are typically enacted and enforced by municipalities, your initial target may not be in Town Hall.

Find out who is paying for the road construction. If it is a private businessperson—for example, a storeowner who is widening his driveway—you should approach him first. Perhaps he does not live or work in the area and is unaware how loud the noise has become, or how long it's continued. In the interests of goodwill (and potential customers) he may act without further ado.

If the noise is caused by municipal road work, your target is clear: the mayor and town council are obviously responsible for obeying their own ordinance. In the case of a county or state project, you may get faster results by going directly to those officials than by asking the town to intervene on your behalf.

Bid Protests

Who issued the original request for proposal (or invitation to bid)? That contracting agency is your initial target. Don't worry about purchasing officials taking offense at your complaint; it is their job to safeguard the integrity of the process.

Should your dispute remain unresolved at the agency level, state procurement regulations will determine where you go next. (Note: whether the award was based on a proposal or a bid, this action is generally called a "bid protest.")

Tools

Basic Principles

Both written and alternative tools can be wielded effectively in each of these situations. In fact, you may put yourself at a disadvantage by neglecting any of the tools available to you.

A letter to your target, whether or not it is required, is an excellent place to start. The writing task itself will force you to work at explaining the problem clearly, logically, and unemotionally. You will need to gather documentation anyway, and the sooner you get it done, the less likely you are to lose, forget, or misfile something. (Because certain supporting materials can play a critical role in tax appeals, nuisance complaints, and bid protests, you need to make sure the materials are received, reviewed, and logged. Generally, it is safer to send hard copies with a postal letter than to attach scanned documents to an email.)

Once written, your letter can then be converted to testimony for, say, an appeals board or a contract dispute mediator. It also lays the groundwork, and establishes your talking points, for personal meetings. If you must deal with similar problems in the future, your letter becomes a template to use again and again.

Personal meetings are not only expected but usually encouraged by the officials involved in these matters. Your lobbying experience will pay off nicely now; you have already learned how to use a face-to-face opportunity productively, efficiently, and persuasively. Be sure to bring any materials that can help the decision-maker understand or evaluate your case. Also, unless you are told that the meeting will be recorded or transcribed, it is wise to take notes.

Phone calls have limited effectiveness in appeals and protests, except to gather information or arrange appointments. However, you can certainly request status reports, follow up on meetings, and confirm the receipt of letters and documents by phone.

Specific Rules and Processes

Tax Appeals

In most jurisdictions, you must either file certain forms or schedule a meeting with an assessor. Usually, you are encouraged to do both. Feel free to compile more documentation than what is required, but watch out for time limits.

Caution: the rules for appealing the assessment of a commercial property may differ from the rules that apply to a home. Be sure to get the correct forms (and the right advice).

Nuisance Complaints

Here you can choose your tools based on your target. A fellow business-person may respond to an informal phone call. If not, you have the option of filing a police report, then attaching it to a letter. It is always a good idea to keep a separate, written record of whom you contacted and when.

If the road work is a municipal project, it may be enough to call the mayor. You can also get fast results by attending a public meeting of the governing body. Explain the problem, give dates and locations, and (firmly but politely) request relief.

Bid Protests

Typically, you will be expected (or required) to meet with the con-tracting agency as well as to put your concerns in writing. The process is designed to encourage dialogue and a good-faith effort on both sides to quickly resolve the dispute. Check on acceptable formats; some jurisdic-tions will allow protests to be emailed or faxed. At the other extreme, you may need to deliver the paperwork in person. Work fast, as deadlines are typically very tight.

If you cannot get satisfaction at the agency level, or there is some extenuating circumstance, you will likely be scheduled for a hearing or mediation by a third party. This could include higher-ranking officials from the same agency, representatives of another agency, or a judge.

Message Tactics

Basic Principles

On the surface, these three challenges might seem to warrant different messages. But fundamentally, they all come down to the issue of equity. So there is a consistent, straightforward message frame: you are seeking evidence-based assessment, even-handed procurement, and proper enforce-ment (of nuisance ordinances) in the interest of fairness to all citizens and businesses.

There are three other similarities. First, you will need to be your own mes-senger, at least in the initial stages of each challenge. Second, comprehen-sion is not a given: you must be careful to use appropriate terminology and formats. Third, documentation is critical. In these situations, no one will—or, indeed, should—take the assertions of any interested party on faith.

Be prepared for vigorous opposition. While less likely to materialize against your tax appeal or nuisance complaint, it is almost inevitable in a bid protest. In all three situations, however, you will strengthen your message by anticipating potential counterarguments.

Finally, watch your tone. Whatever the merits of your case, no official will be moved by self-righteousness or sarcasm. Also, if you lose your temper, it's easy to stray from your message and undermine your own persuasiveness.

Specific Rules and Processes

Tax Appeals

To convince an official that your property is overassessed, you must provide up-to-date, objective evidence. For example, you might show:

- Inaccuracies in the description or valuation of the property.

  Assessors can overlook or unintentionally misrepresent some feature of a building or lot. They could fail to detect structural deterioration or defects. They might also measure incorrectly or make simple arithmetic mistakes. The burden is on you to identify such errors.

- Similar properties in similar neighborhoods with current assessments lower than yours.

- Recent sales of similar properties in similar neighborhoods at prices below your assessment.

  For a rental property, you will also have a record of income derived from the property. A decline in this income may help bolster your case. So could the opinion of an appraiser or other real estate professional.

- Value-reducing factors like neighborhood pollution, traffic hazards, flooding, crime, or blight.

Feel free to buttress your message with photos, repair bills, police records—even media reports.

TRY IT

Does your local assessor update his records on a fixed schedule each year? If so, ask if you could supply him with pertinent information about your property at the appropriate time. By being proactive, you might head off future problems.

Nuisance Complaints

This message is simple: everyone must obey the law. In fact, if you encounter resistance to solving the noise problem, you can make the point by giving your target a copy of the ordinance.

Should you need to ramp up the pressure, call the police. In some communities, an alternative is to request a mediator from the district attorney's office.

A DIFFERENT ANGLE

Question:

You have learned of a loophole in the town's current nuisance ordinance that means it does not apply to your property. Are you now without recourse?

Answer:

As long as you can document an inequity or injustice, there is always some form of recourse. Immediately write a letter to town officials, complaining not only about your situation but also about the need to eliminate the loophole. Follow up by calling or emailing each decision-maker. Better yet, plan to speak at their next public meeting; ask for a commitment to amend the ordinance as well as help in solving your problem.

Bid Protests

There are different types of protests, varying with the level of government, the nature of the product, and many other factors. But all of them, in one way or another, must communicate why the basis for the award was unfair. Here are a few potential reasons:

• The contracting agency did not adhere to the specifications or evaluation criteria stipulated in the bid or proposal documents.

- The bid or proposal documents were ambiguous, incomplete, deceptive, or otherwise flawed.
- The bid specifications violated a law or regulation.
- There were improprieties—like favoritism or collusion—in the process.

Whatever the details of your message, make sure it is thoroughly documented, tightly argued, and filed on deadline. Your oral presentation is important in a contract protest, so build in some time to rehearse.

A DIFFERENT ANGLE

Question:
Can you protest the award of a no-bid contract?
Answer:
Yes. But you may find yourself in murky waters. While competitive contracts must be awarded in accordance with fixed and documented procedures, no-bid contracts can be awarded for reasons that are subjective and loosely defined. This makes it very difficult to pinpoint—let alone prove—some error or impropriety.

As a first step, put your concerns in writing, bring them to a meeting with the contracting officer, and ask him for further guidance.

Learn the Language

You will find these challenges less daunting if you familiarize yourself with some specialized vocabulary. Here are examples of terms related to each.

Tax Appeal Terms

1. Assessment Notice
The assessor issues this yearly document to inform owners of his dollar estimate of their property's value for tax purposes. The notice usually includes a time period during which the assessment may be contested.

2. Equalization
This process attempts to ensure that property is appraised fairly in comparison to the market value of similar property. Whether implemented by

a specialized board of equalization or by some other body, it includes a mechanism allowing owners to contest the municipality's assessment.

3. Informal hearing

Depending on where you live, you may be offered the opportunity of an "informal hearing" on your appeal. Some people worry that this proceeding is less rigorous or conclusive than if it were "formal." By all means, you should ask your assessor; but usually, this descriptor simply means that the outcome can't automatically be appealed to a higher court of law.

4. Millage rate

This is an amount per $1,000 of value applied to your assessment to establish how much you must pay in property tax. The millage rate is set annually by your town.

5. Revaluation

This is a periodic market analysis and comparative valuation of all properties within a municipality (or other jurisdiction). Contrary to conventional wisdom, it does not mean an automatic tax increase. Whether your own assessment goes up or down depends on how it compares to the average change across your town.

Nuisance Complaint Terms

1. Abatement

An action taken to control an offending behavior or condition is called an abatement. For example, noise abatement in many neighborhoods is achieved by establishing "quiet hours" during which construction is prohibited and operation of heavy equipment is curtailed.

2. Cure

Violations of municipal nuisance codes are serious business. Unless an abatement is agreed upon by all parties, the offender may be assessed significant fines and other penalties until the condition has been "cured," or eliminated.

Bid Protest Terms

1. Contracting or procurement officer

This individual has the authority to enter into, administer, and/or terminate contracts on behalf of a government entity. He will probably be your first and most important contact during the proceedings.

2. Interested party

You are only eligible to protest a contract award if you are in a position to derive some economic benefit (or suffer economic harm) from the outcome. This status makes you an "interested party."

3. Price competition

In public contracting, legitimate competition is deemed to exist only when (a) two or more bids or offers are received in response to advertising or formal negotiations, and (b) the award was made to the lowest responsible bidder.

4. Procurement debriefing

After a contract award, some purchasing agencies meet with unsuccessful bidders to answer questions and explain the decision. The goals are to foster trust in the system and to educate vendors. Debriefing may be voluntary or mandatory.

5. Solicitation

This term refers to the process used to communicate procurement specifications and to invite responses from potential vendors. It is sometimes challenged on the basis of how, when, or where the information was disseminated.

The Three Biggest Myths About Tax Appeals, Nuisance Complaints, and Bid Protests

You Will Get Nowhere Unless You Hire an Attorney

Most of these processes are specifically designed to be accessible without an attorney, at least in the initial stages. There are exceptions: for example, commercial property tax appeals in your state may require legal representation unless the owner is a sole proprietor. You might also need a lawyer to resolve an ongoing contract dispute. Still, in all of these situations, you should be able to do a good deal of the legwork yourself.

The Fight Will Cost More Than It's Worth

This second myth is related to the first. You will not be forced to hire a lawyer—or to rack up huge legal bills if you do. While there are filing fees, postal costs, and other procedural expenses, most are minor. More importantly, the Internet has eliminated once-burdensome copying costs for a vast array of critical documents.

All These Processes Are Rigged Against the Little Guy

A public servant is judged by the integrity of his office. Rigging the system is against his own interests, unless he is corrupt—and in that case, sooner or later he will get caught. A "big guy" who fails to do the research, prepare the evidence, or obey the rules will fare no better than anyone else who is careless or disrespectful.

Summary: Dos and Don'ts for Tax Appeals, Nuisance Complaints, and Bid Protests

Do:
- Make sure you understand the rules and procedures.
- Keep written records of whom you contacted and when.
- Be careful to use appropriate terminology and formats.

Don't:
- Expect anyone to "take your word for it."
- Be surprised by opposition, especially to a bid protest.
- Lose your temper.

A Final Note

Your lobbying effort can boost your bottom line whether or not you get the decision, vote, or contract you hoped for. That's because of all you have acquired and experienced along the way. For example, you have gained insights into your community's needs that can generate future product or marketing ideas. You've made contacts with a wide range of new people: potential customers, vendors, and partners. You have raised the profile of your business and of issues that are important to its success.

More specifically, an experienced lobbyist is:

- Savvy about how government works.

    Your future lobbying needs and opportunities are impossible to predict. Officials or agencies that seem irrelevant today could become critical to your business tomorrow. But when you have learned to open doors at one level of government, it is infinitely easier to navigate another. While the nature and scope of the issues will be different, the basic processes—and paths to influence—are largely the same.

- On top of changing laws and regulations.

    For better or worse, almost all public policies evolve over time. Now that you know where and how to find information, you can be vigilant in tracking and responding to changes that directly affect your business.

- Unfazed by powerful officials.

    In lobbying, attitude matters. Timidity and insecurity show, and can undermine the most polished presentation.

    But the more you interact with officials, the easier it is to stand up to them. You will get accustomed to striking just the right balance between respect for their positions and confidence in your own.

Finally, as your lobbying efforts begin to bear fruit, you will become known as a mover and shaker—someone who has the ear of important people. It is hard to quantify the benefits of this kind of reputation, but you'll know them when you see them. Colleagues will seek your advice; politicians will court your support. Will your profits increase? Time will tell. But meanwhile, you can bank what you have already earned: heightened influence, improved confidence, and a persuasive voice in the halls of power.

Appendix

Checklist for a Personal Meeting

Plan, Agenda, and Talking Points for a Personal Meeting

Introductory Letter to a Contracting Agency

Online Resources

For Small Businesses Seeking Government Contracts

For General Information About U.S. Government

Sample Laws, Policies, and Forms

Gift Restrictions

Pay-to-Play Laws

Public Comment Policies

Freedom of Information Form

Vendor Disclosure Form

TIP SHEETS

How to Work a Public Meeting

You can attend a public meeting solely to observe an official or public body in action. But it is also an excellent opportunity to get noticed and begin to establish yourself as a "point person" on your issue—a readily accessible resource for ideas and feedback.

To make the most of this opportunity, take these steps:

1. Arrive before the beginning of the meeting and stay to the end—don't come just for the public portion. Sit near the front.

2. Before the meeting is called to order, introduce yourself informally to the officials and their key staff. Distribute business cards.

3. Introduce yourself to members of the press. Again, offer cards.

4. Plan to participate during the public comment period. Ideally, you should come prepared with a written statement or talking points, but you can also listen to the proceedings with the intent of raising questions or stating your reaction.

5. Be succinct and polite, but leave no doubt that you know what you are talking about.

6. It's fine to come to meetings alone, but a sure way to make an impression is to start bringing others along. If you appear to be the leader or organizer of a group—even a small one—you will become a magnet for the officials' attention.

How to Address a Public Body

Perhaps you plan to deliver testimony to a committee of the state legislature. Maybe you intend to speak during the public comment portion of your town council meeting. In Chapter 2, you learned the basics about addressing a public body. But whatever the occasion and whomever the audience, you can benefit from these extra logistical and stylistic suggestions:

1. If there is advance sign-up for speaking slots, be sure to take advantage of it. Controversy can erupt unexpectedly, and the list of speakers may become so long that some must be cut. Those who signed up early are more likely to get to the microphone.
2. It isn't always best to be first. If you expect an opponent to speak at the same meeting, try to sign up for a slot later than his so you can respond to his arguments.
3. Reporters often leave public meetings early. If you want media attention, try to speak—and to make your key points—while they are still in the room.
4. Even if you are on the friendliest, most informal terms with the officials you are addressing, err on the side of formality while addressing them. You never know how public testimony will sound to others, and it can never hurt to demonstrate respect for the process and the institution.
5. Be sparing with jokes. While it can be helpful to lighten the mood, remember that government is serious business.
6. If there is a microphone, use it even if you have a loud voice. Some mikes are not meant for amplification, only for recording.
7. Don't ask a rhetorical question unless you are prepared for a response. For example, if you ask "Do you know that businesses are going bankrupt in our town?" the mayor might reasonably say, "No, I don't know. Tell me which businesses and when they failed."
8. When speaking before a public body, you don't have to be perfect. You just have to be audible—and accurate.

How to Hold a Press Conference

Let's say you have breaking news to share with the media—information too timely and fast-moving to be relegated to a press release. In that instance, you can call a press conference. But be careful to use this high-urgency technique only if you're sure the story merits it. A reporter might attend one media event out of curiosity, but he'll avoid future ones if he feels you wasted his time or overpromised.

Here are 10 pointers for holding a press conference:

1. Target those reporters who most often write about your town, issue, or type of business. Call them, or a news editor, in advance to find out what time of day would fit into their schedules.

2. Choose a location that is easy to find. Make sure it is protected from inclement weather.

3. Think about your logistical and audio-visual needs. Is there a podium? A microphone? Arrange to test any special equipment well before the press conference begins.

4. Compile a "press kit." Typically, this will include your talking points, background information, any supplemental material—like maps or photographs—and your business card. Decide who will be responsible for distributing press kits to all attendees.

5. Prepare a rough script. While you should not read it to reporters word-for-word, it will help you organize your thoughts and remember key points.

6. Rehearse answers to reporters' likeliest questions. Review previous stories on the subject to get a sense of what they might ask.

7. Expect the unexpected. A press conference is an opportunity for reporters to catch you off guard—which some will deliberately try to do. If you get a question you're truly unable to answer, it's better to decline comment than to bluff or guess.

8. Invite friends and supporters to join you. They don't need to speak, but their presence will boost your confidence.

9. Call reporters the day before your press conference to remind them of the place and time and urge them to come. It's also a good idea to email a media advisory.

10. If reporters don't show up, it doesn't mean they have no interest. Last-minute assignments often disrupt their plans. Simply reschedule as quickly as possible.

Dos and Don'ts When a Government Official Visits Your Premises

Remember the old joke, "I'm from the IRS and I'm here to help you"? Obviously, a tax collector is rarely welcome. But sometimes, a visit by an official actually is beneficial. It can go a long way toward solving problems and building relationships.

Whether the purpose of the visit is routine (like an inspection or assessment) or out of the ordinary (like a customer complaint), treat it as an opportunity instead of an intrusion. Recognize that as long as the official is on your turf, you can pull out all the stops to demonstrate your knowledge and credibility. Here are the basic dos and don'ts:

Do:

- Welcome the official and offer to accompany him.
- Make sure you understand the purpose of the visit.
- Provide in-depth answers to his questions and be forthcoming with additional pertinent information.
- Be friendly and respectful at all times.
- Request a copy of his notes and/or any records he will file after the visit.

Don't:

- Obstruct his access to any part of your premises. (If there are safety concerns, say so.)
- Act resentful or suspicious.
- Complain about government intrusiveness.
- Be obsequious or make attempts to curry favor. (In particular, do not offer gifts!)
- Take the visit as a personal affront. As suggested above, view it as a relationship-building opportunity.

Realistically, your visit may not go well. Depending on what went wrong, it may result in a code enforcement action ranging from an informal warning to an official notice of violation. While local ordinances and mechanisms differ, your first priority should always be to avoid making the situation worse.

Do:

- Respond immediately. Some code violations can trigger daily fines and other penalties that accrue until the situation has been corrected.

- Get all relevant information. At a minimum, the regulatory department or enforcement agency should be able to tell you:

  1. the exact nature of the alleged violation
  2. how it was measured or otherwise ascertained
  3. what your options are (payment of a fine, hearing, mediation, other adjudication mechanisms)

- Review any records or information you gave the visiting official to make sure there were no omissions or errors.

If you received a legal order, compelling you to take some corrective action which is extremely burdensome, expensive, or (in your view) unfair, consult an attorney.

Don't:

- Panic. Even if the violation is serious, most local government authorities will make every attempt to work with you. It is in no one's interest to threaten the long-term viability of your business.

Setting Expectations for Your Lobbying Effort

Remember: in lobbying as in business, no one wins every time. It is important to set realistic goals to avoid getting discouraged or overly cynical. Especially if you've never lobbied before, here are five reasonable but meaningful measures of progress:

Goal #1: Getting Attention

By using the tools and techniques recommended in this book, you will get the right official to focus on the right issue—yours. Even if the result is not what you hoped, it matters that you have learned how to break away from the pack.

Goal #2: Getting Serious Consideration

Government decision-makers do not give equal weight to every opinion or devote the same amount of time to every request. Realistically, they can't—there are just too many advocates and too much information. It is a real accomplishment when you have earned their respect enough to ensure serious consideration of your point of view.

Goal #3: Opening Doors

Your first foray into lobbying may or may not achieve exactly what you want. But it will surely open doors that can lead to new knowledge, long-term relationships, and future opportunities. For example, your advocacy for downtown parking might not produce more spaces—but could get you appointed to an influential small business development task force.

Goal #4: Building Confidence

Few inexperienced advocates feel comfortable in the halls of power. No matter how successful you are in business, the world of government is rife with unique challenges. The best way—indeed, the only way—to develop savvy and self-assurance in lobbying is to do it.

Goal #5: Identifying Allies

It is gratifying to learn that you have allies you never knew, in businesses, neighborhoods, or organizations you never thought of. This is one of many valuable though intangible returns on your lobbying investment: discovering that you're not alone.

A final thought: when evaluating the outcome of your lobbying effort, focus on how far you've come. While there may still be a long way to go, you've found the right road and established critical momentum.

How to Follow Up and Keep Your Effort Alive

It is almost a law of nature: if you don't follow up with your target, your problem/request/issue will end up shunted to a back burner. The falloff in attention isn't personal—it is simply what happens when an official gets inundated by daily demands (and deafened by squeaky wheels).

How can you keep the pressure on without alienating the official or her staff? Here are five suggestions:

1. Set a specific day and time for a weekly follow-up call or email (or both). Be courteous and friendly, but consistent. This will ensure that your issue is regularly revisited by your target or her staff. Importantly, it will send a message to her that you are not going away!

2. If the office of your target is convenient to your home or place of business, consider stopping in, with or without an appointment, just to request a status report. (Don't show up unannounced more than once a week, however; it's not helpful to come across as a pest.)

3. If you obtain new information, documents, or media reports concerning your issue, pass these materials along to the official. Include a personal note.

4. If you have developed a relationship with any reporters, follow up with them too. Make sure they know that your effort is still active and you continue to be available as a source.

5. Recruit other businesspeople, customers, or employees—especially if they are constituents of the same official—to make calls or send emails on your behalf.

No Excuses

If you have the sense that an official is giving you the run-around, he probably is. Don't hesitate to call him on any of these delaying tactics to get the answer you need:

1. Assuring you that he will "look into it."
This can be a legitimate promise—but only if he commits to getting back to you within a specific, reasonable period of time.

2. Changing the subject.
If the runoff from a new county road is flooding your driveway, it doesn't help for the official to wax poetic about the road's benefits. Turn the conversation back to what matters to you.

3. Playing dumb.
Unless you have made a serious targeting mistake, it strains credulity when an official claims no knowledge of an important issue. Call his bluff: offer to provide him with as much information as he wants, as quickly as he wants it.

4. Blame-shifting or finger-pointing.
This is a way of shirking responsibility. Point out that while your problem may have been caused by someone else, it is now his to solve.

5. Claiming he needs to "run it by some other people."
It's fine for the official to ask others' advice, but not for you to be left in limbo. If he doesn't have the authority to make a decision, find out who does—and switch your lobbying focus to that individual.

On the other hand, sometimes an official might recommend going slow for the sake of prudence, or potential advantage. Here are examples of a few good reasons to be patient:

1. The political situation is in flux.
Your target knows more than you do about impending moves on the chessboard of local politics. For instance, if he were to hint of a power shift or other likely development that would strengthen his hand in resolving your issue, it is worth pulling your punches—at least until the picture becomes clearer.

2. A key law or policy is about to change.
Many statutes and regulations "sunset"—automatically lapse—or become subject to modification after a defined period of time. If your target believes that such an imminent change could help you, he is probably right.

3. Additional funds may become available.
Does your request involve some expenditure of public funds? Even when the amount is small, your target will be in a stronger bargaining position if you can wait until the beginning of the government's fiscal year than if he must fight for what's left at the end.

4. The media are showing an interest in your issue.
Even one short story in an influential newspaper might be enough to change your lobbying prospects (for better or worse). Multiple stories could dramatically alter the political landscape. In either case, it makes sense to let the media play its collective hand before you take action.

If All Else Fails . . .

Hopefully, it won't happen to you. But some lobbyists encounter officials (or staff) who are a disgrace to their communities. They might be discourteous, rude, incompetent, untrustworthy—even dishonest. Let's say you have done everything right, only to have an experience gone totally wrong. What should you do?

1. Send a letter to the official documenting your bad experience. Include names, dates, and details. If you get an apology, be gracious (and open-minded) enough to accept it.

2. With an elected official, you have the option of complaining to business groups that have endorsed or financially supported him. Copy his office on your correspondence. Assure him that you will remind these groups about your bad experience close to election time.

3. Complain to the media. All public officials, elected or not, are highly sensitive to criticism in the press.

4. If you suspect criminal wrongdoing, immediately contact law enforcement authorities. Document and provide as many specific details as you can.

5. Don't get discouraged. If this official shows remorse, approach him again. Otherwise, target someone else.

Don't Waste Your Money

There is no shortage of hucksters who try to take advantage of inexperienced lobbyists. Watch out for:

- Consultants of any stripe (including attorneys) who "guarantee" they can deliver a particular government action.
- Products, like directories or databases, that are nothing more than compendiums of free public information.
- "Educational seminars" that are thinly-veiled attempts to sell such products.
- Solicitations for donations to scholarly-sounding foundations or institutions that are actually fronts for political groups.
- Subscriptions to newsletters, magazines, online "courses," or other materials offered by such groups.

Also avoid these unnecessary purchases:

- Recording devices
  The regular sessions of most public bodies are routinely recorded or transcribed. You should be able to get access to the audiotapes and other materials at no charge (there would be a fee for making copies).

- Overnight delivery
  Unless you must deliver a legal document on deadline, it is a waste to pay for any type of rush delivery. In a busy government office, no one will jump to attention (or even notice) when your material arrives.

- Fancy binding or printing

  Content, not cosmetics, is the key to a persuasive advocacy document. Of course, your material should look organized and professional, but expensive trimmings will not help your case.

- Food or drink

  Whether or not there are applicable gift restrictions, it is unnecessary to ply an official with treats. In fact, it can be counterproductive if she gets the impression that you are extravagant—or trying to buy her help.

- Parking

  Urban public buildings are often located in congested downtown districts. Even rural government facilities frequently run short of parking space. Sometimes it is necessary to pay for a private garage, but you should always inquire in advance if there is a free or a low-cost public lot within a reasonable walking distance.

MODELS

Press Releases and Media Advisory

Press Release #1: Announcing an Event or Initiative

—Restaurateurs to Sponsor "Unhappy Hour"—

On April 2, 10 Main Street restaurants will host an "Unhappy Hour" at the Downtown Club to protest the city's new beverage tax. The public is invited between 5–6 PM to learn about the impact of the tax. Free soft drinks will be served.

Jane Smith, spokesperson for the restaurants, said "This tax will force all of us to cut our payrolls and reduce our operating hours. It could drive some of us out of business. We want our customers to know that they could lose some of their favorite spots for local entertainment."

Smith encourages the public to "get educated and get involved" by urging the mayor to repeal the tax. For more information, visit one of the participating restaurants or call 800-111-1111.

Notes

When announcing an event or initiative, make sure to cover:

- What is being announced
- Who is sponsoring it

- Why it matters
- Where the event will take place
- When it will take place
- How to get more information

Media Advisory: Inviting Press to an Event

—Event Notification: "Unhappy Hour"—

What: 10 Main Street restaurants are sponsoring this protest against the beverage tax.
Where: Downtown Club
When: April 2, 5–6 PM
Contact: Jane Smith at 800-111-1111

Note:

A media advisory is simply a reminder to the press that they are invited to attend your event. There is no need to provide additional detail.

Press Release #2: An Opposing Position

—Smith Predicts Restaurant Failures: Calls for Repeal of Tax—

Jane Smith, spokesperson for 10 Main Street restaurants, today called on Mayor Jones to repeal the city's new beverage tax. "This tax is a severe burden on our businesses and could cause some of us to close our doors," said Smith.

The restaurateurs will speak against the tax at the April 10 City Council meeting. All residents, especially patrons of local restaurants, are encouraged to attend.

They will also sponsor "Unhappy Hour," a community protest and educational session. For more information, call Smith at 800-111-1111.

Notes

When writing a release to state opposition, be sure to:

- Identify yourself.
- State what you oppose and what remedy you seek.
- Give reasons.
- Provide next steps.

Press Release #3: A Supporting Position

—Smith Supports Tax Moratorium—

Jane Smith, spokesperson for 10 Main Street restaurants, today thanked the mayor for imposing a moratorium on the new beverage tax.

"We expressed our concerns to the mayor, and he listened," said Smith. "We appreciate his responsiveness."

Smith believes the moratorium will encourage the city to identify an alternative source of revenue. "We have offered to work with the mayor to find creative budget enhancements," she stated.

Mayor Jones commented, "I welcome the restaurateurs' support and look forward to working with them in the interest of all city residents."

Notes

When writing a release to state support, be sure to:

- Identify yourself.
- State what you support.
- Give reasons.
- Provide next steps.
- If appropriate, offer the relevant official an opportunity to be quoted in your press release. He will appreciate your recognition—and the positive media coverage.

Letters or Emails to an Official

Letter #1: Expressing a Position on an Issue

Dear County Commissioner Jones:

I am the owner of Smith Patio Shop, a small business with a proud history in this county. I am writing to share my concern about your proposal to cut funding for the county's Small Business Advisory Center.

When I opened my shop, the SBAC was an invaluable source of advice and education. At that time, I could not have afforded to pay for the services SBAC provided for free. According to the center's records, at least 500 other successful county businesspeople have benefited from its help. I am sure that many more will need it in the future.

In light of your strong record in economic development, I am hopeful that you will reconsider this proposal. I look forward to your response.

Sincerely,
John Smith
10 Tenth Street
Little Town, Your County
Phone: 222-222-2222
Email: smith@email.address

Points to remember:

- It is important to establish up front that (1) you are a constituent and (2) you have credentials and/or experience relevant to this issue.
- Be positive.
- Cite sources for any data.
- If you want to hear back from Commissioner Jones about whether or not he will reconsider his proposal, you must say so. Otherwise, many officials will assume that a response to this kind of letter is unnecessary.

Mistakes to avoid:

- Don't assume the commissioner knows who you are or where you live.
- Don't address more than one issue at a time.
- If you make a vague, unsubstantiated argument, you will get a vague, unsubstantiated response.
- Avoid making accusations, demands, unfounded generalizations, or unrelated complaints.

Letter #2: Requesting Help

Dear Mayor Brown:

I am the owner of Smith Patio Shop at 10 Tenth Street. I am writing to ask for your help with a serious traffic issue.

As you know, Tenth Street is a major east-west thoroughfare. The posted speed limit is 40 miles per hour, but big trucks routinely ignore it. This is a hazard to customers, who are afraid to pull out of my driveway. It also endangers pedestrians and law-abiding drivers. Attached are recent photos of these dangerous conditions.

It is critical to enforce the speed limit and promote safe driving on Tenth Street. I will call your office next week to discuss what can be done.

Thank you in advance for your help.

Sincerely,
John Smith
10 Tenth Street
Phone: 222-222-2222 (Best time to call: Monday–Friday 9–11)
Email: smith@email.address

Points to remember:

- Be brief in explaining your problem, but provide enough detail to enable the official to begin working on it. If your letter includes attachments, identify them.
- Make it clear that you intend to follow up (and be sure to do so!).
- Provide not only your contact information, but also days/times when you can be reached.

Mistakes to avoid:

- Don't assume the official has (or should have) prior knowledge of your problem.
- Don't point fingers.
- It is counterproductive to insist that there is only one acceptable solution to the problem.

Letter #3: Requesting a Meeting

Dear Alderman Good:

I am writing to request a meeting with you at your earliest convenience to discuss the Tenth Street reconstruction project.

The project is directly in front of my store, at 10 Tenth Street. I have done my best to adapt to the temporary inconveniences. However, the chemical odors are becoming intolerable. I want to share with you some contaminated fabrics that you can smell for yourself.

I am available any day next week from 10–5:30, but because the problem is getting worse, I hope we can meet no later than Wednesday. I will call your office at 9:00 a.m. on Monday to arrange a time.

Thank you in advance.

Sincerely,
John Smith
10 Tenth Street
Phone: 222-222-2222 (Best time to call: Monday–Friday 9–11)
Email: smith@email.address

Points to remember:

- Explain the problem.
- Be clear about why you wish to meet (rather than discussing the matter over the phone, for example).
- If there is some urgency to the meeting, mention it.
- Provide your contact information, but specify a time when you intend to follow up.

Mistakes to avoid:

- Don't insist on a particular day or time for the meeting unless there is an emergency or you truly have no choice.
- While the official's staff may take the initiative and call you, it's better not to count on it.

Testimony for a Public Meeting

Testimony #1: An Opposing Position

Thank you for the opportunity to testify on this proposed legislation, which would place new restrictions on how fuel oil can be stored and transported by businesses in our state.

My name is Jane Smith. I own a fuel oil distributorship with residential, commercial, industrial, and government customers. My business will be seriously harmed if you enact the proposed restrictions.

The restrictions will not protect the environment, because we already use airtight, tamper-proof containers and specially reinforced trucks.

The restrictions will not promote energy conservation, because we will need to make more frequent, less efficient deliveries.

The restrictions will:

- increase my costs
- slow my service
- hurt my customers
- force me to lay off employees.

I respectfully ask that you show your concern for small businesses like mine by voting no on this bill. I would be happy to answer any questions.

Note:

Bring enough copies of your testimony (and business cards) to share with every official and member of the press.

Testimony #2: A Supporting Position

Thank you for the opportunity to testify in favor of this proposed ordinance, which would allow home-based businesses in residential neighborhoods.

My name is John Smith. I am a Web designer with an office currently located at 10 Main Street.

My business is quiet, clean, and unobtrusive. I have only one employee. When I meet with clients, it is usually on their premises, so my operation does not cause parking problems or traffic.

Based on my involvement with the City Alliance for Home-Based Workers, I know that many businesses in this community are similar to mine. If we could work full time from our homes, it would allow us to significantly cut our costs and pass on those savings to our customers. It would also contribute to a cleaner environment because would reduce unnecessary car trips and energy consumption.

Home-based businesses are good neighbors. I have brought copies of a recent county report showing that complaints to code enforcement officers and police actually declined last year in neighborhoods where at least 15 percent of residents work from home.

I respectfully ask that you help local home-based businesspeople by enacting this ordinance. I would be happy to answer any questions.

Note:

If possible, bring copies of any reports or other source documents you refer to.

Telephone Scripts

Script #1: Expressing a Position on an Issue

Hello, my name is John Smith. I live at 10 Tenth Street in Little Town. I would like to speak to County Commissioner Jones.

If your call is routed to an aide:

Thank you for taking my call. I am concerned about the Commissioner's proposed cut in funding to the Small Business Advisory Center. Please tell the Commissioner that there are at least 500 county businesspeople like me who have benefited from the services of the SBAC since it opened. I urge him to reconsider this proposal.

If your call is routed to voicemail:

Same as above, but repeat your name and phone number, and offer times when you can be reached.

If your call is routed to the Commissioner:

Thank you for taking my call. I am concerned about your proposal to cut funding to the Small Business Advisory Center. May I take a few minutes now to explain how the SBAC helped me?

If he says yes, give details and offer to answer questions.

If he says no, ask when you could call back.

End the conversation:

There are at least 500 county businesspeople like me who have benefited from the services of the SBAC since it opened. I hope you will reconsider.

Script #2: Requesting Help

Hello, my name is John Smith. I live at 10 Tenth Street in Little Town. I'm calling about a problem with the County Office of Deed Registration. Can the Commissioner help me?

If your call is routed to an aide:

Give a complete explanation of your problem. Get the aide's name and ask when you can expect to hear back from him (or another staff person).

If your call is routed to the Commissioner:

Thank him for taking a personal interest in your problem. Give a complete explanation; ask who you should expect to hear back from and when.

If your call is routed to voicemail:

Give a brief outline of your problem. Repeat your name and phone number and offer times when you can be reached.

In all cases, follow up with an email summary of your conversation.

Op-eds

Supporting a Position

Our community stands at a crossroads. We can decide to change with the times and boost the economic opportunities for our citizens—or to stagnate and drive taxpayers away. The key to moving forward is the proposed update to the zoning code, which would allow home-based businesses in most residential neighborhoods.

According to data from the county office of economic development, the number of sole proprietorships in our region has increased by 40 percent. There are also more professionals in solo practice than ever before.

The county realtors' association has found that houses already zoned for limited commercial use—e.g., home offices—are worth, on average, 30 percent more than comparable properties located in residence-only zones.

Opponents of the change claim that it will mean more traffic, pollution, and crime. But our town's independent businesspeople draw most of their customers from the local area. They prosper when the town prospers, so they have a strong stake in the integrity of their neighborhoods.

Within a 50-mile radius, there are highly successful models of small businesses and residents not only coexisting in harmony, but actually being helpful to each other. In Small Town, street crime went down when more professionals were allowed to work regularly out of their homes. In Little Place, home businesspeople joined with their neighbors to start up a series of block parties and street fairs.

In April, 20 local business owners formed a coalition called Home Business Leads the Way. In just two weeks, our petition drive collected hundreds of signatures from throughout the town.

We hope you will join our effort—and potentially increase your own property value. Please visit our Web site, www.zoningforhomebiz.org, to learn more, sign the petition, and help build a brighter future for our community.

Notes:

- Pick two or three points to be the heart of your argument.
- Provide context for your facts.
- Use specific examples.
- Make a personal connection where possible.
- To boost your chances of getting published, keep your focus local; the newspaper isn't looking for national columnists.
- While some publications are more restrictive than others, you will usually be safe if you stick to a 750–800 word limit.

Responding to Opposition

The debate about changing Home Town's zoning and building code has heated up in recent weeks. Unfortunately, this is because the issue has been politicized by some local candidates.

Our restrictive and cumbersome code is not a problem just for one political party. It is a problem for all current residents, and a deterrent to potential new residents. Those who characterize our reform proposal as a "political ploy" are seriously misinformed.

Today's code was written decades ago, when our town had sparse commercial development. There was so much open land that no one could imagine a time when no space would be left and office rents would be the highest in the eastern part of the state. But that has happened; and now, entrepreneurs and sole proprietors, whose numbers are exploding in the region, cannot afford to start or run their businesses here. These enterprising individuals are moving to other towns, or deciding not to locate here in the first place. This means they are creating jobs and generating revenue elsewhere.

It is not constructive to blame this situation on "short-sighted leadership by the party in power." The truth is that none of our officials in either party foresaw the pace of development or the changes in the regional economy. It is wrong to suggest, as our opponents do, that reform would only mask other problems and boost the image of a few politicians.

Here is what reform would accomplish. By loosening restrictions on home-based businesses, it would make property in Home Town attractive to a wider variety of prospective buyers. This would increase the value of residential real estate by an estimated 30 percent. By streamlining the permit process for commercial construction, it would encourage expansion and renovation of existing office buildings and ultimately strengthen our tax base.

See for yourself. An economic analysis of our proposal by a professor at HT University is posted on our Web site, www.zoningforhomebiz.org.

Most importantly, don't allow our economic future to be hijacked for partisan gain.

Notes:

- Don't make generalized attacks on the opposition; stay focused on your issue.

- It's not enough to assert that the opposition is wrong; you must explain why.

- Keep your argument specific and evidence-driven. Use quotes to home in on points you need to refute.

- Strong, evocative language is acceptable; vitriol and personal slurs are not.

Letters to the Editor

Supporting a Position

Dear Editor,

Thank you for your recent editorial in favor of changing the zoning code to allow home-based businesses in residential neighborhoods.

In addition to the information in your recent stories on this subject, readers should know that the change would be a major boost to local property values. According to the county realtors' association, houses already zoned for limited commercial use—e.g., home offices—are worth, on average, 30 percent more than homes located in residence-only neighborhoods.

There is a petition drive underway to support the zoning change. Readers are urged to visit our Web site, www.zoningforhomebiz.org, to sign on and learn more.

Susan Jones, President
Home Business Leads the Way

Notes:

- State up front why you are writing.
- Establish a connection to any related news stories, editorials, or letters that have appeared in the same publication.
- Provide one or two new facts or arguments; don't repeat material the newspaper has already printed.
- End by telling interested readers what they can do or how to get more information.
- Be as brief as possible.

Responding to Opposition

Dear Editor,

I am writing in response to the letter writer who recently claimed that our organization's proposal to reform the zoning and building code is "politically motivated."

Nothing could be further from the truth. We are not affiliated with any candidate or political party. More importantly, we don't want citizens to be distracted or confused by this misguided attack. There are only two real issues:

- Our reform plan has the potential to boost property values by 30 percent.
- By changing the current code, we can attract new businesses, create jobs, and strengthen Home Town's tax base.

We encourage readers to learn more by visiting our Web site, www.zoningforhomebiz.org.

Susan Jones, President
Home Business Leads the Way

Notes:

- State upfront what or who you are responding to.
- Explain briefly why your opponent is wrong.
- Restate one or two of the key arguments in favor of your position.
- Try to avoid sounding defensive.
- Tell readers how they can get more information.

Petition

A Petition to the Mayor and Council of Hometown

We, the undersigned taxpayers, request revision of the zoning code to allow home-based businesses in residential neighborhoods. We believe this change will boost the resale value of our homes while broadening the tax base of our community. We call on you to take this action immediately.

Name	Address	Phone/Email

Points to remember:

- If you are filing a statutory petition, be sure to research all formatting and other rules.
- Unless a statute says otherwise, you may include as many lines as you wish on each page. But be sure that signatures (and especially addresses) are legible enough to be verified.

Mistakes to avoid:

- Don't make multiple requests in the same petition.
- Don't forget to target a specific individual or body. A petition addressed to no one will get the attention of no one!

Freedom of Information Letter

Note:

Many jurisdictions have their own forms (usually available online) for submitting these requests. They may be optional, but sticking to the preferred format may get you a quicker response.

Dear [Relevant Official],

This is a request under the freedom of information law in our state. [Use the name of your state statute if you know it: for example, the Sunshine Law or the Open Public Records Law.]

I would like to [inspect, obtain a copy, or otherwise access] the following material:

[Provide as complete a description as possible of the document or record you seek. The more specific you are—names, dates, titles, topics—the faster the processor can retrieve the material. It is not necessary to explain why you want it.]

If there is a copying fee or other charge associated with this request, please inform me in advance at 111-111-1111. [This is important. An overly broad request can trigger exorbitant costs. You can head off the problem if you know about it early enough.] Also inform me when I can expect to receive the material. [Freedom of information laws require government bodies to respond within a specified time frame.]

Should this request be denied, please provide an explanation in writing. [The purpose of obtaining a written rationale is to enable you to challenge the denial, if it appears to be unfair or in violation of the FOI law in your state.]

Thank you for your attention to this request. If you need additional information, please contact me by phone or email. [Give the best times, during regular business hours, when you can be reached].

Sincerely,
Jane Smith
[Provide postal mail and email addresses, telephone, and fax.]

Checklist for a Personal Meeting

Presentation Materials

Documents

#1 (description) ___

#2 (description) ___

#3 (description) ___

Supplements

Photos ___

Maps ___

Other ___

Equipment

Laptop ___

Easel ___

Other ___

Who Is Coming

Confirmed (names) _____

Unconfirmed (names) _____

Leave Behind Materials

Fact Sheet ___

Petition ___

Sample constituent letters ___

Business cards ___

Other ___

Plan, Agenda, and Talking Points for a Personal Meeting

Plan

1. Jane will introduce each member of our group, then distribute fact sheets to all participants. (1–2 minutes)
2. Bob will present the history of the issue. (2–3 minutes)

3. Jane will go into detail on the current situation while Sue coordinates the PowerPoint presentation on her laptop. (8–10 minutes)

4. Bob will explain our specific requests. (5 minutes)

5. Question-and-answer. (open-ended)

Agenda

A. Introductions

B. History

C. Current status—PowerPoint presentation

D. Our requests

E. Questions

Notes:

- The plan is not for distribution. It is simply a tool to help you organize your material and decide in advance who among your group will be responsible for what tasks.

- Note the times assigned to each task. While these are estimates, their purpose is to discourage rambling, long-winded presentations.

- Someone should be in charge of setting up and/or operating any special equipment.

- There should a clear delineation between the background/discussion portions of the meeting (1–3) and the "ask" (4). The idea is to carefully set a stage for your specific requests, instead of introducing them up front without a rationale or context.

- The agenda should be handed out to everyone as soon as they are seated. (Remember to bring enough copies!) Review it briefly so the official and her staff will know what to expect. They are much less likely to interrupt the flow of your presentation if they understand how you have structured it.

Talking Points

- Home Town is the only municipality in a 50-mile radius that still prohibits home-based businesses in all residential neighborhoods.

- This current restrictive zoning decreases property values and discourages solo professionals and entrepreneurs from moving to or staying in our community.

- According to the county office of economic development, the number of regional sole proprietorships has increased 40 percent in the past three years.
- The county realtors' association found that houses zoned for limited commercial use (e.g., home offices) are worth, on average, 30 percent more than comparable homes in residence-only zones.
- Both of our neighboring towns, Small Town and Little Place, have a long-term record of success and few problems with home-based business zones.
- Our organization would be pleased to help promote the importance of changing Home Town's zoning code to allow home-based businesses in most residential neighborhoods.

Note:
This can also be used as a leave-behind fact sheet.

Introductory Letter to a Contracting Agency

Dear Ms. Procurement Official:

I am writing to introduce myself and my services. I am a longtime resident of Home Town as well as an energy audit professional with 10 years of experience helping companies save money.

Having read of the town's efforts to seek energy efficiencies by retrofitting old buildings, I wanted to inform you that my firm has developed a specialty in this area. In a recent local project, we achieved thousands of dollars in monthly savings for the historic HT Hotel simply by modernizing wall insulation and roof tiles.

While I have not worked in the public sector, I am fully licensed by the state Department of Energy. I am also a certified participant in the U.S. Small Business Administration's 8(a) Business Development Program.*

You will be interested to know that my business partner also resides in Home Town. Both of us serve on the municipal board of United Way and are active in a range of local philanthropic endeavors. We have a strong commitment to the well being of our community.

To better acquaint you with our approach and enable us to fully understand your needs, I would appreciate an opportunity to meet with you

---

*The 8(a) Business Development Program offers training, counseling, and other targeted supports to small disadvantaged firms. Contact your local SBA office for application forms and procedures.

and other town representatives. I will call your office next week to arrange an appointment.

Attached is a brochure about our company and two recent news stories about our innovative audit system. Should you wish to check references prior to our visit, please feel free to call:

(1) Mr. Jim White, CEO, HT Hotel 111-111-1111

(2) Mr. Joe Brown, Chief Engineer, Area Supermarkets 222-222-2222

(3) Ms. Ann Black, Facilities Manager, Nearby Store 333-333-3333

Sincerely,
Paul Vendor

Notes:

- If your business holds any SBA-recognized designation or special status (such as women-, minority-, or veteran-owned), it is a good idea to make the official aware of it up front. You may be qualified to compete for state or local set-asides.
- Be sure to mention relevant government certifications. This is especially important if you need to get on a list of vendors pre-qualified to perform a particular type of work.
- When all else is equal (or nearly equal), local government officials like to do business with local people. Stress your community roots and perspective.
- Follow up when you said you would.
- Your letter should be no longer than one page, but you may attach multiple marketing materials.
- Include references (preferably from the local area).
- Keep a record of what you sent to whom.

ONLINE RESOURCES

For Small Businesses Seeking Government Contracts

Business.gov

This U.S. government site provides basic information, including a "Government Contracting Guide," and links to state and local e-commerce and procurement sites.

SBA.gov

The U.S. Small Business Administration offers a wide range of tools and resources, including vendor databases, training opportunities, and financial assistance.

OSDBU.gov

The Office of Small and Disadvantaged Business Utilization Directors Interagency Council sponsors trade shows, vendor outreach events, and educational programs.

GSA.gov

The U.S. General Services Administration's Office of Small Business Utilization promotes increased access to government contracts for small, minority-, and women-owned businesses.

FedBizOpps.gov

This service of the U.S. Government Printing Office lists notices of pending contract awards over $25,000, sales of government property,, and other procurement information, updated daily.

NASPO.org

While primarily aimed at government buying professionals, the site of the nonprofit National Association of State Procurement Officials offers unique products like "Supplier Guide CD: How to Do Business With the States" and its flagship publication "State and Local Government Procurement: A Practical Guide" (available for purchase).

CCR.gov

Central Contractor Registration is the primary registry for companies wishing to do business with the federal government. It is also the home of the Dynamic Small Business Search vendor database.

EPP.gov

The site of the Environmentally Preferable Purchasing program of the U.S. Environmental Protection Agency publicizes federal procurement opportunities for vendors of "green" products (biobased, recycled, and energy efficient).

NIGP.org

The National Institute of Governmental Purchasing administers one-day seminars and a Government Contractors Certificate program for those seeking in-depth training in public sector contracting laws, policies, and practices.

Businessmatchmaking.com

This public-private project is sponsored by the Service Corps of Retired Executives together with several large corporations. It sponsors regional face-to-face selling and training events as well as an online network and Small Business Directory.

Aptac-us.org

The Association of Procurement Technical Assistance Centers is a nation-wide network of government purchasing professionals offering free or low-cost educational programs, outreach events, and individual, confidential counseling. A search tool can locate the PTAC nearest you.

For General Information About U.S. Government

USA.gov

This is the official Web portal of the U.S. Office of Citizen Services and Communications.

LOC.gov

In addition to an unrivalled collection of official government records and publications, the site of the Library of Congress offers THOMAS (thomas.loc.gov), a free congressional bill summary and tracking service.

Note:

Some state legislatures have created programs modeled on THOMAS to facilitate the tracking of state legislation. Inquire at your state's Office of Public Information or Legislative Services.

ThisNation.com

This is a compendium of timely news articles and educational materials about government and politics. The site also offers a free, downloadable textbook focused on federal institutions and processes.

LWV.org

The League of Women Voters of the U.S. is a national nonpartisan grassroots advocacy network. Through its Education Fund, the League provides an array of educational and training resources. This site links to League chapters on the state, county, and municipal levels which often provide local information and publications.

Votesmart.org

Project Vote Smart compiles nonpartisan information about voting records and issue positions based on extensive surveys of elected officials and political candidates at every level of government.

Lib.umich.edu/govdocs

The University of Michigan Documents Center is a clearinghouse for statistical data, news, and publications about local, state, and federal government.

Lpig.org

The Law and Policy Institutions Guide provides a repository of legal information, resources, and directories, including links to state statutes and codes.

SAMPLE LAWS, POLICIES, AND FORMS

Gift Restrictions

Almost every state imposes some restrictions on gifts from paid lobbyists to lawmakers. In most cases, the statute cites a maximum allowable dollar value for any gift.

Some states also limit gifts from unpaid advocates, and extend the rules beyond legislators to all "public officials." Many local governments have their own prohibitions or guidelines; often, these are stricter than state mandates.

There is wide variation among these rules—which means it is critical to check which, if any, apply to you. These examples illustrate the diversity:

• Connecticut: Prohibits gifts exceeding $10 per occasion or $50 in the aggregate for a calendar year.

- Georgia: Prohibits "any gratuitous transfer to a public officer . . . in the amount of $101 or more."
- Michigan: Prohibits gifts exceeding $25 in any one-month period.
- Oregon: Prohibits any gift "with an aggregate value in excess of $100."
- Pennsylvania: Prohibits "anything which is received without consideration of equal or greater value."
- New York City: Prohibits any gift worth $50 or more from a person or firm doing business with the city.

This summary language in Oregon's statute offers one of the more comprehensive definitions of the goal of gift restrictions—however imperfectly that goal may be achieved:

> No public official or candidate for office or a relative of the public official or candidate shall solicit or receive, whether directly or indirectly . . . any gift or gifts . . . from any single source who could reasonably be known to have a legislative or administrative interest in any governmental agency in which the official has or the candidate if elected would have any official position or over which the official exercises or the candidate if elected would exercise any authority.

Sources: National Conference of State Legislatures, www.ncsl.org. New York City Conflicts of Interest Board, www.nyc.gov/ethics.

Pay-to-Play Laws

The colloquial term "pay-to-play" refers to the practice of giving campaign contributions or other benefits to public officials (allegedly) in return for votes, decisions, access, and favors. Laws to restrict such contributions are proliferating both on the state and local levels. For the most part, current pay-to-play laws focus largely on businesses (including professionals, like lawyers or architects) currently holding or seeking government contracts.

When researching applicable laws in your state, here are some key issues you need to explore, with examples of current state practices:

1. Do the restrictions apply only to holders of certain kinds of contracts?
Restrictions may apply only to holders of no-bid contracts, as in Colorado and South Carolina. However, Connecticut, Ohio, and New Jersey

(with some exceptions) restrict holders of both no-bid and competitive contracts.

2. Do the restrictions apply only to holders of contracts above a certain value?

In South Carolina, West Virginia, Kentucky, and Hawaii, all public vendors are subject to pay-to-play restrictions regardless of contract value. But there is a substantial range: in Colorado, restrictions apply only to contracts above $100,000.

3. Which officials are subject to the restrictions?

Again, there is a wide range in current laws. Some are limited to candidates for state offices; others affect candidates for both state and local offices. In Colorado, the restrictions are extended even to school board candidates.

4. What amounts of money—if any—are businesses allowed to give to political candidates subject to the restrictions?

Permitted contributions range from zero to $5,000. There are also timing rules; for example, West Virginia and Illinois prohibit any political contribution from the start of negotiations until the contract's termination.

5. What are the penalties for violating pay-to-play laws?

The most common penalties include contract cancellation and fines. Some states also suspend eligibility for new contracts and revoke business licenses.

Warning: Pay-to-play legislation is in a constant state of flux. If your business is affected, be sure you are on top of the latest developments in your state, county, and municipality.

Source: National Conference of State Legislatures, www.ncsl.org.

Public Citizen, www.citizen.org.

Public Comment Policies

While every local government has its own set of procedures, there will always be clear parameters for public comment during regular meetings of a governing body. Usually, the rules are more restrictive in large cities than in small towns.

Here is a comparison of fairly typical rules governing key procedures in three municipalities of different sizes:

Procedure	Minnetonka, MN (pop. 51,759)	Irvine, CA (pop. 212,793)	Virginia Beach, VA (pop. 433,746)
To address an agenda item.	No special restriction.	No special restriction.	Must register with the city clerk prior to the meeting.
To address a topic not on the regular (noticed) agenda.	No special restriction.	No special restriction.	Unless sponsored by a member of the city council, must make a request in writing prior to the meeting.
Time limit	None.	Three minutes.	Three minutes.
Identification/ disclosure requirement.	Must state name and address at the podium.	Must fill out a speaker's card and submit to the city clerk during the meeting.	In addition to prior notification, must state name, address, and whom the speaker represents.

Note:

In most cases, the mayor or other presiding officer has the authority to grant exemptions from some or all of these requirements. Under certain circumstances, he can also curtail or extend the public comment period, or postpone it to another meeting.

If you wish to testify at a state legislative committee hearing or other meeting of state lawmakers, contact the staff in advance to ask about specific procedures. There can be substantial variation, not only from state to state but often among committees in the same legislative body.

A word of caution when planning a day at the Statehouse: arrive early and be prepared to stay late. Unless you plan to address a very low-profile body on an obscure topic, there will almost certainly be more speakers than you expect. Also, keep in mind that the legislators will probably call on state or local officials to testify ahead of you, even if you arrived earlier than they did. Fair or not, this practice is a common form of professional courtesy.

Freedom of Information Form

Federal law mandates citizen access to public documents at every level of government. While there is no standard FOI form currently in use, it is helpful to be familiar with a typical format.

The forms are designed to encourage specificity in FOI requests. They also attempt to clarify whether the request is for document inspection, reproduction, or both. Importantly, look for disclosure of copying fees and other potential charges (for tasks such as sorting, compiling, tabulating, or summarizing information).

Keep in mind that even if you are required to complete a form, you have the option of writing a letter to further explain or more thoroughly document your request.

Here is an idea of what you can expect:

Town of Little Place

Freedom of Information Request Form

Date:

Requestor:

Name _____
Address _____
Contact information _____

Information requested:

Please be as specific as possible. Provide enough detail to enable us to efficiently identify and locate the correct records/documents.

_____
_____

Type of access requested:

Please indicate if you wish to

– Inspect records/documents _____
– Copy records/documents _____
– Both inspect and copy records/documents _____

If you wish to copy records/documents, please choose a format:

– Paper
– CD, diskette, or other computer-readable copy
– Other (explain _____)

Pursuant to state law, you will receive a response to this request within seven days. If our office requires an extension, you will be notified. Should your request be denied, you are entitled to a written explanation.

Please note that the FOI Act allows municipalities to charge (at the rate of $ .25 per page) for the costs of reproduction and/or processing. Delivery and postage fees are additional. Any anticipated costs in excess of $10.00 must be paid in full before records/documents will be released.

I wish to be notified of anticipated costs before such costs are incurred: Yes __ No __

Vendor Disclosure Form

Where required of potential vendors, the purpose of these forms is to uncover and document potential conflicts of interest before a contract is awarded. While differing widely in scope, emphasis, and format, the most common areas of emphasis include:

1. Identification of all public officials and employees who could financially benefit from the contract.
2. Disclosure of any existing business or familial relationships between your company and any public official or employee in the jurisdiction where you are seeking a contract.
3. Disclosure of political contributions by principals in your company to local political candidates, party organizations, or other partisan entities.

Here is a typical format:

Town of Little Place

Vendor Disclosure Form

Vendor's name and address:
Name and title of person completing form:
This form is provided with:

Invitation to Bid _____ Request for Proposal _____ Contract _____ Other (explain) _____

Pursuant to state law, you are required to disclose the name and address of all public officials/employees in the jurisdiction of Little Town:

(1) With whom you, members of your family, or any of your employees have a family or personal relationship, and who may benefit financially (or in another substantive manner) from the proposed transaction.

(2) Who currently hold an interest in your business (including employment).

Name of official/employee   Address

_____   _____

_____   _____

Describe below any financial or other substantive benefits that could be gained by these officials/employees as a result of the proposed transaction.

_____

_____

You are also required to disclose all political contributions by owners or officers in your company to candidates or partisan organizations in Little Town over the 12 months prior to submission of this form.

Name of recipient   Date of contribution   Amount of contribution

_____

_____

The undersigned is authorized to provide this information and certifies its accuracy:

Signature_____

Notes

INTRODUCTION

1. National Small Business Poll (2003). National Federation of Independent Business Research Foundation, Vol. 3(1), http://www.nfib.com.

2. Ibid.

3. Bergan, Daniel (2009). "Does Grassroots Lobbying Work? A Field Experiment Measuring the Effects of an E-Mail Lobbying Campaign on Legislative Behavior," *American Politics Research* Vol. 37(2), 327–52.

4. Gordon, Jim (2009). "Hey, Look Us Over: Gardiner Jockeys for a Piece of the Action," *Westchester County Business Journal*, June 3.

TARGET

1. Rivera, Ray, and Russ Buettner (2008). "Speaker Says Council Allotted Millions to Fake Groups and Spent It Elsewhere." *New York Times*, April 4: C9.

2. Massachusetts Public Interest Group (2008). "Transparency.gov 2.0: Using the Internet for Budget Transparency to Increase Accountability, Efficiency and Taxpayer Confidence." http://www.masspirg.org, December

3. Pritchett, Rachel (2007). "Bainbridge Mayor Gets Emotional Over Angry Public Comment." *Kitsap Sun*, October 11.

4. Symons, Michael (2009). "Clerk Can Charge $460,000 for OPRA Request," *Asbury Park Press*, http://www.app.com, April 28.

5. Samuels, Michael (2008). "Nassau Eyes a Business Boom." *Long Island Business News*, December 2.

6. Estes, Andrea (2009). "Retailers Can't Get, or Give, Tax Break." *Boston Globe*, August 16 B1, 5.

7. Messina, Judith (2006). "Biz Owners Fight Back." *Crain's New York Business*, October 9.

8. Edwards, Haley Sweetland (2009). "Maplewood Businesses Share Worries." *New York Times, The Local blog*, http://www.nytimes.com, April 10.

9. Ziegler, Elizabeth (2009). "SLC Council Considers Options for Unpopular Business Fee Increase." KCPW 88.3 FM, June 1.

10. Cheslow, Jerry (2005). "Loving the Landscape, But Not the Sprawl." *New York Times*, February 27.

11. Sulzberger, A. G. (2009). "Yoga Faces Regulation, and Firmly Pushes Back." *New York Times*, July 11.

TOOLS

1. Meissen, Roger (2009). "Eminent Domain Petitioning to Return to a Street Corner Near You," *Fulton Sun*, January 23.

2. Kamshoshy, Sarah (2007). "Plaza Proposal Sparks Controversy," *Daily Californian*, February 8.

3. Baldwin, Carly (2009). " 'We'll Help You Leave Hoboken'—Controversy Swirls Around Billboard," *Jersey Journal*, March 24.

MESSAGE TACTICS

1. Shifrin, Simon (2009). "Proposal Would Triple Cost of Food Licenses," *Idaho Business Review*, February 9, http://www.idahobusiness.net.

2. Levin, Irwin, and G. Gaeth (1988). "How Consumers are Affected by the Framing of Attribute Information Before and After Consuming the Product," *Journal of Consumer Research* 15 (December), 374–78.

3. Arora, Raj (2000). "Message Framing and Credibility," *Health Marketing Quarterly* 18 (1/2), 29–43.

4. Meyerowitz, Beth, and S. Chaiken (1987). "The Effect of Message Framing on Breast Self Examination Attitudes, Intentions and Behavior," *Journal of Personality and Social Psychology* 52 (March), 500–10.

5. California Chamber of Commerce (2008). "2008 Small Business Advocate of the Year Award Winners," http://www.calchamber.com, November 26.

6. Loewy, Tom (2008). "Food Safety Violations Rising in County," *Galesburg Register-Mail*, http://www.galesburg.com, May 12.

7. Campanile, Carl (2009). "Schools Get Back to the Data-Basics," *New York Post*, May 25, 2.

OTHER CONSIDERATIONS

1. U.S. Committee for Economic Development (2005). "Building on Reform: A Business Proposal to Strengthen Election Finance," http://www.ced.org.

2. Viser, Matt, John Drake, Michael Levenson, Jonathan Saltzman, and Andrew Ryan, (2008). "Wilkerson Vows to Stay in Race, Criticizes U.S. Attorney," *Boston Globe*, http://www.boston.com, October 29.

3. Winzelberg, David (2008). "LI Realtors Get Political by Hosting Voter Registration," *Long Island Business News*, September 12.

4. FBI Report (2008), "Fraud and Corruption: Stemming the Surge," http://www.fbi.gov.

5. Lockwood, Jim (2009). "Not Guilty Plea in Bid to Bribe Mayor," *Star Ledger*, April 2, 15.

6. Levenson, Michael (2009). "City Gets Refresher Course in Ethics," *Boston Globe*, August 16, B4.

7. O'Brien, Dan (2005). "Cracking Down on Public Corruption: Why We Take It So Seriously . . . and Why It Matters to You," http://www.fbi.gov/page2/june05/obrien062005.htm.

8. Davies, Mark, Esq. (2002). "Addressing Municipal Ethics: Adopting Local Ethics Laws," in Ethics in Government, Albany: New York, State Bar Association, 108.

9. Editorial (2008). *Birmingham News*, http://www.al.com, December 4.

10. Frank, Al (2008). "Prominent Builder Faces Bribery Trial," *Star Ledger*, September 19, 18.

11. Polansky, Risa (2009). "Developers Get Wide Range to Roam for Air Terminal Revamp," *Miami Today*, August 6, 8.

Bibliography

Arora, Raj (2000). "Message Framing and Credibility," *Health Marketing Quarterly* 18 (1/2), 29–43.

Baldwin, Carly (2009). "We'll Help You Leave Hoboken—Controversy Swirls Around Billboard," *Jersey Journal*, March 24.

Bergan, Daniel (2009). "Does Grassroots Lobbying Work? A Field Experiment Measuring the Effects of an Email Lobbying Campaign on Legislative Behavior," *American Politics Research* Vol. 37 (2).

Birmingham News Editorial (2008). *Birmingham News*, December 4.

California Chamber of Commerce (2008). "2008 Small Business Advocate of the Year Award Winners," http://www.calchamber.com, November 26.

Campanile, Carl (2009). "Schools Get Back to the Data-Basics," *New York Post*, May 25.

Cheslow, Jerry (2005). "Loving the Landscape, But Not the Sprawl," *New York Times*, February 27.

Davies, Mark, Esq. (2002). "Addressing Municipal Ethics: Adopting Local Ethics Laws," in *Ethics in Government*, Albany, NY: New York State Bar Association.

Edwards, Haley Sweetland (2009). "Maplewood Businesses Share Worries," *New York Times* 'The Local,' http://www.nytimes.com, April 10.

Estes, Andrea (2009). "Retailers Can't Get, or Give, Tax Break," *Boston Globe*, August 16.

FBI Report (2008). "Fraud and Corruption: Stemming the Surge," http://www.fbi.gov/fraud_corruption.

Frank, Al (2008). "Prominent Builder Faces Bribery Trial," *Star Ledger*, September 19.

Gordon, Jim (2009). "Hey, Look Us Over: Gardiner Jockeys for a Piece of the Action," *Westchester County Business Journal*, June 3.

Holman, C. (2008). "Pay to Play Restrictions on Campaign Contributions from Government Contractors 2007–2008," Public Citizen, http://www.citizen.org.

Kamshoshy, Sarah (2007). "Plaza Proposal Sparks Controversy," *Daily Californian*, February 8.

Levenson, Michael (2009). "City Gets Refresher Course in Ethics," *Boston Globe*, August 16.

Levin, Irwin, and G. Gaeth (1988). "How Consumers are Affected by the Framing of Attribute Information Before and After Consuming the Product," *Journal of Consumer Research* 15 (December), 374–78.

Lockwood, Jim (2009). "Not Guilty Plea in Bid to Bribe Mayor," *Star Ledger*, April 2.

Loewy, Tom (2008). "Food Safety Violations Rising in County," *Galesburg Register-Mail*, May 12.

Massachusetts Public Interest Research Group (2008). "Transparency.gov 2.0: Using the Internet for Budget Transparency to Increase Accountability, Efficiency and Taxpayer Confidence," http://www.masspirg.org, December 3.

Meissen, Roger (2009). "Eminent Domain Petitioning to Return to a Street Corner Near You," *Fulton Sun*, January 23.

Messina, Judith (2006). "Biz Owners Fight Back," *Crain's New York Business*, October 9.

Meyerowitz, Beth, and S. Chaiken (1987). "The Effect of Message Framing on Breast Self Examination Attitudes, Intentions and Behavior," *Journal of Personality and Social Psychology* 52 (March), 500–10.

National Small Business Poll (2003). *National Federation of Independent Business Research Foundation* Vol. 3(1).

New York City Conflicts of Interest Board (2009). "Lobbyist Gift Law," http://www.nyc.gov/ethics.

O'Brien, Dan (2005). "Cracking Down on Public Corruption: Why We Take It So Seriously . . . and Why It Matters to You," fbi.gov Headline Archives. http://www.fbi.gov/fraud_corruption.

Polansky, Risa (2009). "Developers Get Wide Range to Roam for Air Terminal Revamp," *Miami Today*, August 6.

Pritchett, Rachel (2007). "Bainbridge Mayor Gets Emotional Over Angry Public Comment," *Kitsap Sun*, October 11.

Public Citizen (2009). "Pay to Play Restrictions on Campaign Contributions from Government Contractors 2008–2009," http://www.citizen.org.

Rivera, Ray, and Russ Buettner (2008). "Speaker Says Council Allotted Millions to Fake Groups and Spent It Elsewhere," *New York Times*, April 4.

Samuels, Michael (2008). "Nassau Eyes a Business Boom," *Long Island Business News*, December 2.

Shifrin, Simon (2009). "Proposal Would Triple Cost of Food Licenses," *Idaho Business Review*, February 9.

Sulzberger, A. G. (2009). "Yoga Faces Regulation, and Firmly Pushes Back," *New York Times*, July 11.

Symons, Michael (2009). "Clerk Can Charge $460,000 for OPRA Request," *Asbury Park Press*, April 28.

U.S. Committee for Economic Development (2005). "Building on Reform: A Business Proposal to Strengthen Election Finance," http://www.ced.org.

Viser, Matt, John Drake, Michael Levenson, Jonathan Saltzman, and Andrew Ryan (2008). "Wilkerson Vows to Stay in Race," *Boston Globe*, October 29.

Winzelberg, David (2008). "LI Realtors Get Political by Hosting Voter Registration," *Long Island Business News*, September 12.

Wood, Natalie O'Donnell (2009). "Pay to Play: State Reforms," *National Conference of State Legislatures Legisbrief* Vol. 17 (28), http://www.ncsl.org.

Ziegler, Elizabeth (2009). "SLC Council Considers Options for Unpopular Business Fee Increase," Salt Lake City KCPW 88.3 FM, June 1.

Index

About the Author

Assemblywoman **Amy H. Handlin**, PhD currently serves as Deputy Minority Leader of the New Jersey General Assembly. She is also an Associate Professor in the Department of Management and Marketing at Monmouth University. Her experience in public office spans 20 years and multiple levels of state and local government. She holds a BA from Harvard, an MBA from Columbia, and a PhD from New York University's Stern School of Business.